Bible Chronology and Pertinence

T. F. Igler

NEW HARBOR PRESS

RAPID CITY, SD

Igler/New Harbor Press
1601 Mt. Rushmore Rd, Ste 3288
Rapid City, SD 57701e
www.NewHarborPress.com

Ordering Information:
Quantity sales. Special discounts are available on quantity purchases by corporations, associations, and others. For details, contact the "Special Sales Department" at the address above.

Bible Chronology and Pertinence / Thomas Igler. -- 1st ed.
ISBN 978-1-63357-376-5

Preface

CHRONOLOGY AND PROPHETIC UNDERSTANDING go hand-in-glove. Accurate, expressive chronology, properly reported, is commensurate with revelatory eschatology.

The word "mystery" is used repeatedly in New Testament scripture. The principle thought is that those things are precious, typically prophetic and entertained as "hidden truth." Chronology is not only the timeline of Bible history; it is inherent to those mysteries and prophecies believers hold precious. This study does endeavor in that arena.

This study requests a far-reach into the reader's allowance of favor, faith, and regard. A kind of confidence that is agreeable only if the reader perceives the study is flavored with conviction, humility, and confession. Knowing this, things-biblical cannot be entertained or claimed as personal property.

Intellect and objectivism, abiding alone, will not yield the true gift of detail that answers chronology's most difficult questions. Revelatory exposition may be in order. That venture favors both spirituality and subjectivity. However mystical, our intellect would concede to the rank of "ready servant." A kind of simplicity that may be despised.

Spirituality, and its neighbor subjectivity, are integral to this study. Necessarily, subjectivity will be on display. Let not those additions burden the integrity of the whole. Only the needed measure of subjectivity will enter the arena of settlements. "Honest reporting" is a necessary ingredient. Transparency and accountability are the obvious earmarks of a worthwhile writing endeavor. Call it integrity. So that honest reporting be helped along, certain terms are integrated into the account. Statements such as "estimated" and "approximation." Those kinds of declarations are self-explanatory.

Without exception, blind spots appear after the fact. In that light, such an undertaking, if pride-driven, would not happen. It is hoped that the reader grasps the underlying gist of the message. That message, prophetic in nature, is that God has a "Plan." His plan is real, and the plan holds mankind at the pinnacle of his love and regard. God is exacting, and his "Word" will not fail. God's "will" or intent "is the mother of us all."

The shell and meat of "right intent" are to minister good information with reasonable conclusions, having clarity beyond confusion and annoyance. Any other motive lacks due-regard for the reader. Right settlements are realized by humble pursuit and sincere application. The reader is encouraged toward the same subscription.

Contents

Introduction

Humility, patience, and giving careful attention to the Bible narrative complements the claim of "scripture alone." The references are scripture. This does not deny the possible benefit of similar publications. While no such advantage has yielded profit to this chronology, we hold to the proverb, "There is no new thing under the sun." No literature search is required to secure that fact. However humbling, that fact is biblical, and honesty will suffice. Be that as it may; this study attempts toward originality and "solo scriptoria."

Salvation in Christ is the New Testament "message of the kingdom;" yet, the question needs to be presented: Does not God expect, even require, that our hearts desire his revealed truth as to beginnings? At least that part, we are privileged to search out. However arduous the undertaking, the answer should be at least probably yes. All things eternal proceed from one God eternal, and his mind is inclusive of all things from the beginning to the end. As allowed, we desire to have the mind of God. This writing, dealing with "beginnings" and the facts of the Old Testament, gives us a necessary and encouraging glimpse into the pith and marrow of God's Plan of the Ages.

Reading the Old Testament, it's timeline and prophecies are primary—above the price of rubies. Having a heart that embraces chronology and prophecy allows us to better approach God's intentions concerning mankind. This statement, in this introduction, may best reveal the basis of this study and the desire toward sharing this study.

The primary source of this study is the Bible; particularly, an older, well-worn KJV Oxford Bible, with its dictionary, proper scripture names, subject index, and concordance.

The chronology begins with a bare-bones list of item numbers and dates. When dates relate to "prophetic times," then pertinent statements are included.

Repeating of information is evident as the reader goes from section to section. The redundancy is intentional. The purpose: Primarily, the reader is spared the distraction of back-referencing. Also, it is agreed among teachers that repetition is helpful toward the student's grasp and retention of the lesson's overview.

The reference addendum is listed last on the contents page. While it is the heart of this study, it is the "reference" and the 267 items listed are consistent throughout the articles; thus, readily accessed in the back of the book.

CHRONOLOGY:
ITEM NUMBERS WITH DATES

		Year of man	BC
1.	"In the beginning God created the heavens and the earth." Gen. 1:1		
2.	*Adam	0	4000
3.	Abel, first God-conscious son of Adam	unknown	
4.	*Seth born of Adam @ 130	130	3870
5.	*Enos born of Seth @ 105	235	3765
6.	*Cainan born of Enos @ 90	325	3675
7.	*Mahalaleel born of Cainan @ 70	395	3605
8.	*Jared born of Mahalaleel @ 65	460	3540
9.	*Enoch born of Jared @ 162	622	3378
10.	*Methuselah born of Enoch @ 65	687	3313
11.	*Lamech born of Methuselah @ 187	874	3126
12.	Adam died @ 930	930	3070
13.	Enoch died @ 365	987	3013

14.	Seth died @ 912	1042	2958
15.	*Noah born of Lamech @ 182	1056	2944
16.	Enos died @ 905	1140	2860
17.	Cainan died @ 910	1235	2765
18.	Mahalaleel died @ 895	1290	2710
19.	Jared died @ 962	1422	2578
20.	*Shem born of Noah @ 500	1556	2444
21.	Lamech died @ 777	1651	2349
22.	Methuselah died @ 969	1656	2344
23.	FLOOD	1656	2344
24.	*Arphaxad born of Shem @ 102	1658	2342
25.	*Salah born of Arphaxad @ 35	1693	2307
26.	*Eber born of Salah @ 30	1723	2277
27.	*Peleg born of Eber @ 34	1757	2243
28.	*Reu born of Peleg @ 30	1787	2213
29.	The Tower of Babel/Confusion approximate	1817	2183
30.	*Serug born of Reu @ 32	1819	2181
31.	*Nahor born of Serug @ 30	1849	2151
32.	*Terah born of Nahor @ 29	1878	2122
33.	*Abram born of Terah @ 70	1948	2052
34.	Sarai born	1958	2042

35.	Peleg died @ 239		1996	2004
36.	Nahor died @ 148		1997	2003
37.	Noah died @ 950		2006	1994
38.	Abraham and family to Canaan		2023	1977
39.	Rue died @ 239		2026	1974
40.	Abram @ 85 married Hagar		2033	1967
41.	Ishmael born to Abram @ 86		2034	1966
42.	Covenant of circumcision; Abram renamed Abraham		2047	1953
43.	Isaac promised; Sarai renamed Sarah		2047	1953
44.	Circumcision; Abraham @ 99, Ishmael @ 13		2047	1953
45.	Sodom destroyed		2047	1953
46.	*Isaac born of Abraham @ 100		2048	1952
47.	Serug died @ 230		2049	1951
48.	Ishmael cast out @ 20	an approximation	2054	1946
49.	Isaac offered @ 30		2078	1922
50.	Terah died @ 205		2083	1917
51.	Sarah died @ 127		2085	1915
52.	Isaac @ 40 married Rebekah		2088	1912
53.	Arphaxad died @ 438		2096	1904
54.	*Jacob and Esau born of Isaac @ 60		2108	1892

55.	Abraham died @ 175; Isaac @ 75		2123	1877
56.	Salah died @ 433		2126	1874
57.	Esau @ 40 married Hittite women		2148	1852
58.	Shem died @ 600		2156	1844
59.	Jacob @ approx. 62 fled toward Padan-aram First blessing of God at Bethel	estimate	2170	1830
60.	Jacob @ approx. 69 married Leah and Rachel	estimate	2177	1823
61.	*Judah born of Jacob @ 76	estimate	2184	1816
62.	Eber died @ 464		2187	1813
63.	Joseph born of Jacob @ 91		2199	1801
64.	Jacob and family fled from Laban		2205	1795
65.	Jacob dwelt in Shalem an estimated 7 years Put away idols; second blessing at Bethel Name change confirmed Later, Rachael died in childbirth		2212	1788
66.	Joseph @ 17 sold into slavery		2216	1784
67.	Isaac died @ 180		2228	1772
68.	Joseph @ 30 stood before Pharaoh		2229	1771
69.	Jacob @ 130, and family to Egypt (Joseph @ 39)		2238	1762
70.	Begin 430-year Sojourn period		2238	1762
71.	Jacob died @ 147		2255	1745
72.	*Phares, born of Judah @ +99	estimate	2283	1717

73.	Joseph died @ 110		2309	1691
74.	*Esrom born of Phares @ 72	estimate	2355	1645
75.	*Aram born of Esrom @ 72	estimate	2427	1573
76.	*Aminadab born of Aram @ 72	estimate	2499	1501
77.	*Naason born of Aminadab @ 72	estimate	2571	1429
78.	Moses born Begin first 80 of 480 years of 1 Kings 6:1		2588	1412
79.	Moses @ 40 fled Egypt		2628	1372
80.	Caleb born		2629	1371
81.	Joshua born	estimate	2629	1371
82.	*Salmon born of Naason @ 72	estimate	2643	1357
83.	Moses @ 80 spoke to Pharaoh Aaron @ 83 spoke to Pharaoh Egypt judged		2668	1332
84.	Exodus: 14th day, 1st month Later the same year the Law was given End of 430-year Sojourn period		2668	1332
85.	The Tabernacle was reared up; 1st day, 1st month, 2nd year		2669	1331
86.	Israel kept Passover; 14th day, 1st month, 2nd year		2669	1331
87.	Twelve spies search the land		2669	1331

88.	Aaron died @ 123; 1st day, 5th month, 40th year		2708	1292
89.	Moses died @ 120; 11th or 12th month, 40th year		2708	1292
90.	Israel crossed Jordan the 10th day, first month and kept Passover the 14th day, first month; Jericho fell and a curse was pronounced		2709	1291
91.	At rest; end of war; land divided		2714	1286
92.	*Boaz born of Rachab; Father, Salom @ 72	estimate	2715	1285
93.	Joshua died @ 110 years old	estimate	2739	1261
94.	40 years' rest under Othniel; first Judge		2714–2754	1286
95.	8 years' oppression by Cushan	estimate	(2739–2747)	1261
96.	18 years' servitude to Eglon, king of Moab		2754–2772	1246
97.	40 years' rest under Ehud, a Benjamite		2772–2812	1228
98.	20 years' oppression by Jabin, king of Canaan		(2812–2832)	1188
99.	40 years' rest under Barak		2812–2852	1188
100.	*Obed born of Ruth; father Boaz @ 99	estimate	2814	1186
101.	7 years delivered into the hand of the Midianites		(2845–2852)	1155
102.	40 years' rest under Gideon		2852–2892	1148
103.	3 years' usurpation by Abimelech; call it 2891		(2891–2894)	1109
104.	23 years under Tola of Issachar		2894–2917	1106

105.	*Jessie born of Obed @ 90	estimate	2904	1096
106.	Eli born		2912	1088
107.	22 years under Jair, a Gileadite		<u>2917</u>–2939	1083
108.	18 years; oppression by Ammonites		(<u>2921</u>–2939)	1079
109.	6 years under Jephthah, the Gileadite		<u>2939</u>–2945	1061
110.	7 years under Ibzan of Bethlehem		<u>2945</u>–2952	1055
111.	10 years under Eglon, a Zebulonite		<u>2952</u>–2962	1048
112.	8 years under Abdon, a Pirathonite		<u>2962</u>–2970	1038
113.	40 years delivered into hands of Philistines; Samson judged 20 years during the time of Philistines' rule		<u>2970</u>–3010	1030
114.	40 years under Eli		<u>2970</u>–3010	1030
115.	Saul begins 40-year reign as king Beginning of Kings' Dominions		2984	1016
116.	*David born of Jessie @ 90		2994	1006
117.	Philistines take Ark of God, beginning 21 years' absence Eli died @ 98 Decisive Philistine defeat ending 40 years' domination		3010	990
118.	Samuel died	estimate	3024	976
119.	Saul died in battle		3024	976
120.	David @ 30 begins 40-year reign as king, reigning initially in Hebron 7.5 years		<u>3024</u>–3031	976

121.	David reigns in Jerusalem 33 years; After 21 years, Ark of God returned		3031–3064	969
122.	*Solomon born of David @ 40	estimate	3034	966
123.	*Rehoboam born of Solomon @ 29	estimate	3063	937
124.	David died		3064	936
125.	Solomon begins 40-year reign as king		3064	936
126.	Solomon's temple began End of 480-year period of 1 Kings 6:1		3068	932
127.	Solomon's Temple completed; later, the dedication		3075–3076	925
128.	The Dedication; statements of beginnings, glory, and judgment; begin 390 years of Ezek. 4:5		3076	924
129.	*Abijam born of Rehoboam @ 20	estimate	3083	917
130.	Solomon died; Rehoboam reigns initially in his stead		3104	896
131.	Rehoboam @ 41 years begins 17-year reign		3104	896
132.	Nation divides: Judah to Rehoboam, Israel to Jeroboam		3104	896
133.	Jeroboam begins 22-year reign over Israel		3104	896
134.	Jeroboam turns Israel to idol worship		3104	896
135.	Prophecy to Jeroboam and Israel; Josiah mentioned		3104	896
136.	*Asa born of Abijam @ 25	estimate	3108	892

137.	Shishak of Egypt spoiled/claimed some of Judah	3109	891
138.	Rehoboam died	3121	879
139.	Abijam begins 3-year reign over Judah in 18th of Jeroboam	3122	878
140.	Abijam died	3124	876
141.	Asa begins 41-year reign over Judah; 20th of Jeroboam	3124	876
142.	Jeroboam died	3126	874
143.	Nadab begins 2-year reign over Israel	3126	874
144.	Nadab slain by Baasha	3127	873
145.	Baasha begins 24-year reign over all Israel in Tirzah, 3rd of Asa	3127	873
146.	*Jehoshaphat born of Asa @ 23		
147.	Asa calls great offering and makes covenant with God	3139	861
148.	Baasha died	3150	850
149.	Elah begins 2-year reign over Israel in Tirzah, 26th of Asa	3150	850
150.	Elah slain by Zimri	3151	849
151.	Omri begins 6 of 12-years reign in Tirza	3151	849
152.	Omri begins 6-year reign after Tirzah, 31st of Asa	3156	844
153.	*Jehoram born of Jehoshaphat @ 26	3157	843

154.	Omri died		3162	838
155.	Ahab begins 22-year reign over Israel, 38th of Asa		3162	838
156.	Asa died		3165	835
157.	Jehoshaphat @ 35 begins 25-year reign over Judah		3166	834
158.	Jericho rebuilt	approximation	3173	827
159.	*Ahaziah born of Jehoram @ 17		3174	826
160.	Ahab died after being smitten in battle		3183	817
161.	Ahaziah begins 2-year reign over Israel, 17th of Jehoshaphat		3183	817
162.	Jehoram (Joram) begins 12-year reign over Israel		3184	816
163.	Ahaziah died after injury/disease		3185	815
164.	Jehoram @ 32 begins 8-year reign over Judah		3189	811
165.	Jehoshaphat of Judah died		3191	809
166.	Jehoram (Joram) of Judah died, smitten of disease		3196	804
167.	Ahaziah @ 22, reigned 1 year over Judah, 12th of Joram		3196	804
168.	*Joash, son of Ahaziah born @ 23		3197	803
169.	Jehoram (Joram) of Israel died, smitten by Jehu		3197	803
170.	Ahaziah of Judah died, smitten by Jehu		3197	803

171.	Jehu begins 28-year reign over Israel	3197	803
172.	Athaliah begins 6-year rule over Judah	3198	802
173.	Athaliah died, slain by the sword	3204	796
174.	Joash @ 7 begins 40-year reign over Judah	3204	796
175.	*Amaziah, son of Joash, Born @21	3218	782
176.	Jehoahaz begins 17-year reign over Israel, 23rd year of Joash	3224	776
177.	Jehu died	3225	775
178.	Jehoahaz of Israel died	3241	759
179.	Jehoash begins 16-year reign over Israel, 37th of Joash	3241	759
180.	Joash of Judah died	3243	757
181.	Amaziah @ 25 begins 29-year reign over Judah	3243	757
182.	*Uzziah (Azariah), son of Amaziah, born @ 36	3254	746
183.	Jehoash of Israel died	3258	742
184.	Jeroboam begins 41-year reign over Israel, 15th of Amaziah	3258	742
185.	Azariah @ 16 reigns 12 years co-regent over Judah	3261	739
186.	Amaziah died, 15 years after Jehoash of Israel	3273	727
187.	Azariah's reign continued 40 years as sole king of Judah	3273	727
188.	*Jotham, son of Azariah (Uzziah), born @ 36	3290	710

189.	Jeroboam (Israel) died	3299	701
190.	Zachariah reigns 6 months over Israel, 38th of Azariah	3299	701
191.	Zachariah died, slain by Shallum	3300	700
192.	Shallum begins 1-month reign over Israel	3300	700
193.	Shallum died, slain by Menahem	3300	700
194.	Menahem begins 10-year reign over Israel, 39th of Azariah	3300	700
195.	*Ahaz, son of Jotham, born @ 20	3310	690
196.	Menahem died	3310	690
197.	Pekahiah begins 2-year reign over Israel, 50th Uzziah	3311	689
198.	Great Earthquake: Amos 1:1, Zechariah 14:5	3313	687
199.	Isaiah's vision	3313	687
200.	Uzziah (Azariah) died	3313	687
201.	Pekahiah died, slain by Pekah	3313	687
202.	Pekah begins 20-year reign over Israel	3313	687
203.	Jotham @ 25 begins 16-year reign over Judah, 2nd of Pekah	3315	685
204.	*Hezekiah, son of Ahaz, born @ 11	3321	679
205.	Jotham died	3330	670
206.	Ahaz @ 20 years begins 16-year reign over Judah	3330	670

207.	Pekah died, slain by Hoshea	3333	667
208.	Hoshea begins 9-year reign over Israel	3342	658
209.	Ahaz died	3346	654
210.	Hezekiah @ 25 begins 29-year reign over Judah, 3rd of Hoshea	3346	654
211.	Shalmaneser of Assyria besieges Samaria (Israel)	3349	651
212.	Samaria taken; end of northern kingdom (Israel)	3352	648
213.	Hezekiah healed and given 15 additional years	3360	640
214.	Judah besieged	3360	640
215.	*Manasseh, son of Hezekiah, born @ 42	3363	637
216.	Hezekiah died	3375	625
217.	Manasseh @ 12 begins 55-year reign	3375	625
218.	*Amon, son of Manasseh, born @ 45	3408	592
219.	*Josiah, son of Amon, born @ 16	3424	576
220.	Manasseh died	3430	570
221.	Amon @ 22 begins 2-year reign	3430	570
222.	Amon died, slain by his servants	3432	568
223.	Josiah @ 8 begins 31-year reign	3432	568
224.	*Jehoiakim, son of Josiah, born @ 14	3438	562
225.	Jehoahaz, son of Josiah, born @ 16	3440	560

226.	Josiah @ 16 begins to seek God	3440	560
227.	Josiah @ 20, in 13th year begins the purge; Within a year, he fulfills prophecy of 1 Kings 13:2	3444	556
228.	The time of Jeremiah warning *"all the people* *of Judah."* Fulfilled prophecies: 1 Kings 13:2; 2 Kings 23:26–27; Begin 40 years of Ezek. 4:6 and 23 years of Jer. 25:3	3445	555
229.	Josiah initiates final urgent actions, hoping for a remedy	3450	550
230.	Purge completed; great Passover was the 18th year	3450	550
231.	Zedekiah, son of Josiah, uncle to Jehoiachin, born @ 29	3453	547
232.	*Jehoiachin, son of Jehoiakim, born @ 18 *Jeconiah, son of Jehoiakim born @ 18 estimate	3456	544
233.	Josiah died, slain by Pharaoh Nechoh	3463	537
234.	Jehoahaz @ 23 begins 3-month reign	3463	537
235.	Jehoahaz taken by Pharaoh Nechoh; died in Egypt	3463	537
236.	Jehoiakim (Eliakim) @ 25 begins 11-year reign	3463	537

237.	Nebuchadnezzar begins reign as King of Babylon; Jehoiakim refuses to heed Jeremiah's warnings; Nebuchadnezzar supplants the King of Judah as per the judgment of God; the glory departs the nation; end of 390 years of Ezek. 4:5		3466	534
238.	Jeremiah reflects on his warning (Jer. 25:3–11); End of stated 23 years		3467–<u>3468</u>	532
239.	Jehoakim rebels last 8 years of 11-year reign		3466–<u>3474</u>	526
240.	Jehoiakim died		3474	526
241.	Jehoiachin @ 18 begins 3-month reign		3474	526
242.	Beginning of 70-year Babylonian captivity		3474	526
243.	Zedekiah (Mattaniah) @ 21 begins 11-year reign		3474	526
244.	*Salathiel, born of Jeconiah in captivity @ 21	estimate	3477	523
245.	The 5th year of Jehoiachin's captivity; Ezekiel prophesies of 390 days/years, and 40 days/years		3479	521
246.	Jerusalem besieged by Nebuchadnezzar about 1½ year and then destroyed the 11th year of Zedekiah		3483	517
247.	Jerusalem was broken up and burned, taken and occupied; the men of war fled, and the walls and Temple torn down; end of 40 years of Ezek. 4:6		3485	515
248.	*Pedaiah, son born of Salathiel @ 21	estimate	3498	502

249.	Evil Merodach, King of Babylon, begins to reign		3511	489
250.	*Zorobabel born of Pedaiah @ 21	estimate	3519	481
251.	Babylon falls to Darius; Cyrus decrees a return to Jerusalem and to *"build him an house in Jerusalem."* End of 70 years' Babylonian captivity; begin 490 years as prophesied (Dan. 9:24–27)		3544	456

Following: The estimation of forty-three to forty-four years between generations is subject to a more correct, lesser number as per the more complete depiction and explanation of Chart; Christ Lineage, Old Testament Record, Matthew 1 and Luke 3.

252.	That time span of 490 years is 3544 to 4034		3544	456
253.	*Abiud born	estimate	3562	438
254.	*Eliakim born	estimate	3605	395
255.	*Azor born	estimate	3649	351
256.	*Sadoc born	estimate	3692	308
257.	*Achim born	estimate	3736	264
258.	*Eliud born	estimate	3779	221
259.	*Eleazar born	estimate	3823	177
260.	*Matthan born	estimate	3866	134
261.	*Jacob born	estimate	3910	90
262.	*Joseph born	estimate	3953	47
263.	*Jesus born	estimate	3996	4 BC

264. Jesus baptized in Jordan; begin last 7 years of   4027   27 AD
     Dan. 9:27

265. Jesus crucified; Great earthquake;   4030   30 AD
     resurrection middle of the week (Dan. 9:27)

266. *Generation of Christ born at Pentecost   4030   30 AD

267. Stephen stoned and the people scattered; end   4034   34 AD
     of the 70th week (Dan. 9:27);
     end of 490 years of Dan. 9:24–27

CHAPTER 2

CHRONOLOGY; CHRIST LINEAGE

THE LINEAGE OF CHRIST is a priority. The individuals of the lineage and their life dates are noted. Where reasonable and justifiable, "completions" are added. There is no reflection on the fact of the "inerrancy of scripture." Missing dates are reasonably estimated. Those take nothing from the accuracy or continuity of the whole. The estimations are duly noted as such and are within the timeframes of stated or calculated dates. Reasonable time periods of births and deaths relating to the line of Christ could have been left unattended, being an almost insurmountable difficulty. However, that part was included in the study. The matter is reconciled and the lineage given, with lifespans, both accurately determined and estimated. The effort, however subjective in parts, is thought to be complementary toward a more complete chronology. The Reference Addendum and the chart Christ Lineage; Old Testament Record, Matthew 1 and Luke 3 provide added explanation.

2.	*Adam	0	4000
4.	*Seth born of Adam @ 130 130-0=130, age of Adam at son's birth	130	3870
5.	*Enos born of Seth @ 105 235-130=105, age of Seth at son's birth	235	3765
6.	*Cainan born of Enos @ 90 325-235=90, age of Enos at son's birth	325	3675

7.	*Mahalaleel born of Cainan @ 70 395-325=70, age of Cainan at son's birth	395	3605
8.	*Jared born of Mahalaleel @ 65 460-395=65, age of Mahalaleel at son's birth	460	3540
9.	*Enoch born of Jared @ 162 622-460=162, age of Jared at son's birth	622	3378
10.	*Methuselah born of Enoch @ 65 687-622=65, age of Enoch at son's birth	687	3313
11.	*Lamech born of Methuselah @ 187 874-687=187, age of Methuselah at his birth	874	3126
15.	*Noah born of Lamech @ 182 1056-874=182, age of Lamech at son's birth	1056	2944
20.	*Shem born of Noah @ 500 1556-1056=500, age of Noah at son's birth	1556	2444
24.	*Arphaxad born of Shem @ 102 1658-1556=102, age of Shem at son's birth	1658	2342
25.	*Salah born of Arphaxad @ 35 1693-1658=35, age of Arphaxad at son's birth	1693	2307
26.	*Eber born of Salah @ 30 1723-1693=30, age of Salah at son's birth	1723	2277
27.	*Peleg born of Eber @ 34 1757-1723=34, age of Eber at son's birth	1757	2243
28.	*Reu born of Peleg @ 30 1787-1757=30, age of Peleg at son's birth	1787	2213
30.	*Serug born of Reu @ 32 1819-1787=32, age of Reu at son's birth	1819	2181

31.	*Nahor born of Serug @ 30 1849-1819=30, age of Serug at son's birth		1849	2151
32.	*Terah born of Nahor @ 29 1878-1849=29, age of Nahor at son's birth		1878	2122
33.	*Abram born of Terah @ 70 1948-1878=70, age of Terah at son's birth		1948	2052
46.	*Isaac born of Abraham @ 100 2048-1948=100, age of Abraham at son's birth		2048	1952
54.	*Jacob and Esau born of Isaac @ 60 + 2108-2048=60, age of Isaac at son's birth		2108	1892
61.	*Judah born of Jacob @ 76 2184-2108=76, age of Jacob at son's birth	estimate	2184	1816
72.	*Phares born of Judah @ 99 2283-2184=99, age of Judah at son's birth	estimate	2283	1717
74.	*Esrom born of Phares @ 72 2355-2283=72, age of Phares at son's birth	estimate	2355	1645
75.	*Aram born Esrom @ 72 2427-2355=72, age of Esrom at son's birth	estimate	2427	1573
76.	*Aminadab born of Aram @ 72 2499-2427=76, age of Aram at son's birth	estimate	2499	1501
77.	*Naason born of Aminadab @ 72 2571-2499=72, age of Aminadab at son's birth	estimate	2571	1429
82.	*Salmon born of Naason @ 72 2643-2571=72, age of Naason at son's birth	estimate	2643	1357
92.	*Boaz born of Rachab; father Salom @ 72 2715-2643=72, age of Salom at son's birth	estimate	2715	1285

100.	*Obed born of Ruth; father Boaz @ 99 2814-2715=99, age of Boaz at son's birth	estimate	2814	1186
105.	*Jessie born of Obed @ 90 2904-2814=90, age of Obed at son's birth	estimate	2904	1096
116.	*David born of Jessie @ 90 2994-2904=90, age of Jessie at son's birth		2994	1006
122.	*Solomon born of David @ 40 3034-2994=40, age of David at son's birth	estimate	3034	966
123.	*Rehoboam born of Solomon @ 24 3063-3037=24, age of Solomon at son's birth	estimate	3063	937
129.	*Abijam born of Rehoboam @ 20 3083-3063=20, age of Rehoboam at son's birth	estimate	3083	917
136.	*Asa born of Abijam @ 25 3108-3083=25, age of Abijam at son's birth	estimate	3108	892
146.	*Jehoshaphat born of Asa @ 23 3131-3108=23, age of Asa at son's birth		3131	869
153.	*Jehoram born of Jehoshaphat @ 26 3157-3131=26, age of Jehoshaphat at son's birth		3157	843
159.	*Ahaziah born of Jehoram @ 17 3174-3157=17, age of Jehoram at son's birth		3174	826
168.	*Joash, son of Ahaziah born @ 23 3197-3174=23, age of Ahaziah at son's birth		3197	803
175.	*Amaziah, son of Joash, born @ 21 3218-3197=21, age of Joash at son's birth		3218	782
182.	*Uzziah (Azariah), son of Amaziah, born @ 36 3254-3218=36, age of Amaziah at son's birth		3254	746

188.	*Jotham, son of Azariah (Uzziah) born @ 36 3290-3254=36, age of Uzziah at son's birth		3290	710
195.	*Ahaz, son of Jotham, born @ 20 3310-3290=20, age of Jotham at son's birth		3310	690
204.	*Hezekiah, son of Ahaz, born @ 11 3321-3310=11, age at son's birth		3321	679
215.	*Manasseh, son of Hezekiah, born @ 42 3363-3321=42, age of Hezekiah at son's birth		3363	637
218.	*Amon, son of Manasseh, born @ 45 3408-3363=45, age of Manasseh at son's birth		3408	592
219.	*Josiah, son of Amon, born @ 16 3424-3408=16, age of Amon at son's birth		3424	576
224.	*Jehoiakim, son of Josiah, born @ 14 3438-3424=14, age of Josiah at son's birth		3438	562
232.	*Jehoiachin, son of Jehoiakim, born @ 18 3456-3438=18, age of Jehoiakim at son's birth		3456	544
	Jeconiah, son of Jehoiakim born @ 18 3456-3438=18, age of Jehoiakim at son's birth	estimate	3456	544
244.	*Salathiel, born of Jeconiah in captivity @ 21	estimate	3477	523
248.	*Pedaiah, son of born of Salathiel @ 21	estimate	3498	502
250.	*Zorobabel born of Pedaiah @ 21	estimate	3519	481

Following: The estimation of 43 to 44 years between generations is subject to a more correct lesser number as per the more complete depiction and explanation of Chart; Christ Lineage, Old Testament Record, Matthew 1 and Luke 3.

253.	*Abiud born 3519+43=3562	estimate +43	3562	438

254.	*Eliakim born 3562+43=3605	estimate +43	3605	395
255.	*Azor born 3605+44=3649	estimate +44	3649	351
256.	*Sadoc born 3649+43=3692	estimate +43	3692	308
257.	*Achim born 3692+44=3736	estimate +44	3736	264
258.	*Eliud born 3736+43=3779	estimate +43	3779	221
259.	*Eleazar born 3779+44=3823	estimate +44	3823	177
260.	*Matthan born 3823+ 43=3866	estimate +43	3866	134
261.	*Jacob born 3866+44=3910	estimate +44	3910	90
262.	*Joseph born 3910+43=3953	estimate +43	3953	47
263.	*Jesus born 3953+43=3996	estimate +43	3996	4

CHAPTER 3

CHRIST'S LINEAGE; OLD TESTAMENT RECORD, MATTHEW 1 AND LUKE 3

Old Testament Record	Luke 3:23–38
Note: Connecting line indicates agreement.	
Adam	Adam
Seth	Seth
Enos	Enos
Cainan	Cainan
Mahalaleel	Maleleel
Jared	Jared
Enoch	Enoch
Methuselah	Mathusala
Lamech	Lamech
Noah	Noe
Shem	Sem
Arphaxad	Arphaxad
	*Cainan
Salah	Sala
Eber	Heber
Peleg	Phalec

Reu	Ragau
Serug	Saruch
Nahor	Nachor
Terah	Thata

*Cainan, redundant in Luke's record, is reasonably treated as an error in compilation.

Matt. 1:1–16 added to the Old Testament record	Luke's record continues
Abram	Abraham
Isaac	Isaac
Jacob	Jacob
Judah	Juda
Phares	Phares
Esrom	Esrom
Aram	Aram
Aminadab	Aminadab
Naason	Naason
Salmon	Salmon
Boaz	Booz
Obed	Obed
Jessie	Jesse
David	David

At this point, Luke's lineage follows Nathan, and Matthew's follows Solomon. Names in parentheses are of record, whereas Matthew leaves six unnamed.

Solomon	Nathan
Rehoboam	Mattatha
Abijam	Menan
Asa	Melea
Jehoshaphat	Eliakim
Jehoram	Jonan

Asa	Joseph
Ahaziah	Juda
Joash	Simeon
(Amaziah)	Levi
(Uzziah–Azariah)	Matthat
(Jotham)	Jorim
Ahaz	Eliezer
Hezekiah	Jose
Manasseh	Elmodam
Amon	Cosam
Josiah	Addi
(Jehoiakim)	Melchi
Jeconiah (Jehoiachin)	Neri
Salathiel	Salathiel
(Pedaiah)	
Zorobabel	Zorobabel

The divergent lineages come together briefly in Salathiel and Zorobabel.

Going forward, the Old Testament lineage record stops. Going forward, there are eleven persons in the Matthew lineage and nineteen persons in the Luke lineage. Reasonably, there are omissions in Matthew's lineage.

Abiud	Rhesa
	Joanna
Eliakim	Juda
	Joseph
Azor	Semei
	Mattathias
Sadoc	Maath
	Negge
Achim	Esli
	Naum

Eliud

Eleazar

Matthan

Jacob
Joseph
Jesus

Amos
Mattathias
Janna
Melchi
Levi
Matthat
Heli
Joseph
Jesus

CHAPTER 4

CHRONOLOGY; TIME OF THE JUDGES

THIS SECTION OF THE study is a revisit to the time of the Judges. That is the years of man from 2714 to 3010. The text is refreshed for the convenience of the reader. Additional explanations are included. It will be obvious that the forty-year timespans are several, and this "forty-year figure" is given special consideration. Also, it is evident that this study gives place to the idea of "continuity of Jewish leadership" within the nation. The treatment of these two considerations may seem to be overriding factors in determining the "time of the Judges." Confessedly, the student has a right to pause.

Caleb was eighty-five years old when he petitioned for the Hebron land grant. Josh. 14:10-15: *"And now, behold, the LORD hath kept me (Caleb) alive, as he said, these forty and five years, even since the LORD spake this word unto Moses, while the children of Israel wandered in the wilderness: and now, lo, I am this day fourscore and five years old.... Now therefore give me this mountain, whereof the LORD spake in that day... And Joshua blessed him, and gave unto Caleb the son of Je-phun-neh Hebron for an inheritance. ...And the land had rest from war."*

That was the year 2714 (2629+85=2714). Jericho had fallen, and the land had rest from war. The phrase *"and the land had rest"* is associated with a forty-year time frame. In this instance, 2714 to 2754.

Josh. 15:13–17: *"And unto Caleb the son of Je-phun-neh he gave a part among the children of Judah, according to the commandment of the LORD to Joshua, even the city of Arba the father of Anak, which city is Hebron.' ... And Caleb said, 'He that smiteth Kir-jath-se-pher, and taketh it, to him will I give Ach-sah his daughter to wife.' And Othniel the son of Kenaz, the brother of Caleb, took it: and he gave him Ach-sah his daughter to wife."*

Later, after the death of Joshua, as per Judges 1:12–15, the statement is repeated. There is no disparity, being that the account in Judges is an update, or it was the time the matter was concluded.

What is evident is that Othniel enters the leadership picture earlier than thought. The initiation of the contract, with Othniel's inclusion, was in the timeframe of the *"rest"* in the year 2714. Joshua lived twenty-five years beyond this marker. Going forward in this study, Othniel is treated as the person of significance who kept the rest. He is the transition person where the nation enters the "time of the Judges."

We do not know the exact year Joshua was born or the year he died. It is a reasonable conjecture that Joshua and Caleb were in the same age bracket. Joshua was probably younger, but we do not know that. Exod. 33:11 refers to Joshua as *"a young man."* Referring to the same year, post-Exodus, Caleb was forty years old in that first year after the Exodus. Joshua 14:7 states, *"Forty years old was I when Moses the servant of the LORD sent me from Kadesh-bar-ne-a to espy out the land..."* Equating Joshua's age to be the same as Caleb's, we thus estimate Joshua to be thirty-nine years old at the Exodus event 2668, and the year 2629 as his birth (2668-39=2629). Thus, Joshua's death would have been approximately the year 2739 (2629+110=2739). Joshua 24:29 states, *"And it came to pass after these things, that Joshua the son of Nun, the servant of the LORD, died, being an hundred and ten years old."*

93.	Joshua died @ 110	estimate	2739	1261

The children of Israel were free of bondages until the time of Joshua's death and possibly ten years beyond. Josh. 24:31: *"And Israel served the LORD all the days of Joshua, and all the days of the elders that overlived Joshua, and which had known all the works of the LORD, that he had done for Israel."*

The approximation of Joshua's death was thirty years after crossing Jordan into the promised land, 2739 (2709 to 2739=30). It is inferred that the elders that *"overlived"* Joshua were his generation of men. The time of Israel's good behavior ended in the approximation of forty years after entering the promised land, 2749 (2709+40=2749). That would be ten years after Joshua's death (2739 to 2749=10). An obvious exception was the eight years' interruption by Cushan at a time of Israel's discouragement, about the time of Joshua's death. These dates are approximations and could reasonably vary five years.

It is a reasonable conjecture that Cushan of Mesopotamia rose up as Israel vacillated about the time of Joshua's death. So that the year 2739 would mark the estimated beginning of eight years' oppression by Cushan, king of Mesopotamia. That oppression would have been within the ending years of the forty years peacekeeping of Othniel, eight years of oppression from 2739 to 2747. The forty years of rest attributed to Othniel thus included the eight years' oppression, or interruption, by Cushan. That eight years was concluded about the last seven years of Othniel's forty years of rest and then judgeship.

Refreshing the point: As determined earlier, Othniel entered leadership approximately the year 2714, but his deliverance of the nation from the oppression of Cushan was his mark of "judge."

He was God's instrument of rest then deliverance, and he was the person of transition from the law-giver to judge. Going forward, they were judges because their acts of courage and deliverance were statements, judgments, and verdicts as to Israel's dreadful plight. Othniel was peacekeeper and judge forty years (2714 to 2754).

Going from the "Joshua" text to the "Judges" text sees us struggling with difficult determinations. Dates given in Judges are not always consecutive. Necessarily, special attention is given to the narrative. The years of oppression are often given as inclusive of the tenure of the judge-of-record when the Jews failed and were oppressed. Those dates are given in parentheses.

Judges 3:7–9, 11:

And the children of Israel did evil in the sight of the LORD, and forgat the LORD their God, and served Baalim and the groves. Therefore the anger of the LORD was hot against Israel, and he sold them into the hand of Chushan-rishathaim king of Mesopotamia: and the children of Israel served Chushan-rishathaim eight years. And when the children of Israel cried unto the LORD, the LORD raised up a deliverer to the children of Israel, who delivered them, even Othniel the son of Kenaz, Caleb's younger brother... And the land had rest forty years. And Othniel the son of Kenaz died.

94.	40 years' rest under Othniel, younger brother of Caleb.		2714–2754	1286
95.	8 years' oppression by Cushan	estimate	(2739–2747)	1261

The eighteen years' servitude to Eglon, king of Moab, is not included in the years of any Jewish judgeship. Regarding this exception, it is noteworthy that Moab had a kinship with Israel.

Judges 3:12, 14: *"And the children of Israel did evil again in the sight of the LORD: And the LORD strengthened Eglon the king of Moab against Israel, because they had done evil in the sight of the LORD.... So the Children of Israel served Eglon the king of Moab eighteen years."*

96.	18 years' servitude to Eglon, king of Moab		2754–2772	1246

Judges 3:15, 30–31: *"But when the children of Israel cried unto the LORD, the LORD raised them up a deliverer, Ehud the son of Gera, a Benjamite, a man left-handed... So Moab was subdued that day under the hand of Israel. And the land had rest fourscore years. And after him was Shamgar the son of Anath, which slew of the Philistines six hundred men with an ox goad: and he also delivered Israel."*

The words *"the land had rest"* is expressed four times in Judges (3:11, 30; 5:31, 8:28). The forty-year figure is attached to all, excepting this verse, where it is ascribed *"fourscore years."* Nowhere in scripture is such an eighty-year tenure ascribed to one man. A forty-year tenure as judge is acceptable, being the total *"rest"* was eighty years up to that time, including the prior forty years of rest under Othniel. Duly noted, we will give Ehud's judgeship as forty years, not eighty.

97. 40 years' rest under Ehud, a Benjamite   2772–2812   1228

Judges 4:1–3: *"And the children of Israel again did evil in the sight of the LORD, when Ehud was dead. And the LORD sold them into the hand of Jabin king of Canaan, that reigned in Hazor; the captain of whose host was Sisera, which dwelt in Harosheth of the Gentiles. And the children of Israel cried unto the LORD: for he had nine hundred chariots of iron; and twenty years he mightily oppressed the children of Israel."*

This twenty years *"he (Jabin) mightily oppressed the children of Israel"* was within the first twenty years of Deborah's judgeship. *"She judged Israel at the time"* (Judges 4:4).

98. 20 years' oppression by Jabin, king of Canaan   (2812–2832)   1188

Judges 4:4; 5:1–2, 31: *"And Deborah, a prophetess, the wife of Lapidoth, she judged Israel at the time... Then sang Deborah and Barak the son of Abinoam on that day, saying, Praise ye the LORD for the avenging of Israel, when the people willingly offered themselves. So let all thine enemies perish, O LORD: but let them that love him be as the sun when he goeth forth in his might. And the land had rest forty years."*

The forty-years rest included the judgeships of both Deborah and Barak.

99. 40 years' rest under Barak   2812–2852   1188

Judges 6:1: *"And the children of Israel did evil in the sight of the LORD: and the LORD delivered them into the hand of Midian seven years."*

These seven years *"delivered"* into the hand of Midian were in the last seven years of Barak's forty years.

101. 7 years delivered into the hand of the   (2845–2852)   1155
        Midianites

Judges 6:8 to 8:27 gives the narrative of first how a prophet, then an angel, then the faith and obedience of Gideon wrought victory over Midian.

Judges 8:28: *"Thus was Midian subdued before the children of Israel, so that they lifted up their heads no more. And the country was in quietness forty years in the days of Gideon."*

102.   40 years' rest under Gideon   <u>2852</u>–2892   1148

Judges 8:33–9:56.

And it came to pass, as soon as Gideon was dead, that the children of Israel turned again, and went a whoring after Baalim and made Baal-be-rith their god. And the children of Israel re-membered not the LORD their God, who had delivered them out of the hands of all their enemies on every side: Neither shewed they kindness to the house of Jer-ub-ba-al, namely, Gideon, ac-cording to all the goodness which he had shewed unto Israel... And all the men of She-chem gathered together, and all the house of Millo, and went, and made A-bim-e-lech king... When A-bim-e-lech had reigned three years over Israel... Then God sent an evil spirit between A-bim-e-lech and the men of Shechem... Thus God rendered the wickedness of A-bim-e-lech which he did unto his father, in slaying his seventy brethren.

103.   3 years' usurpation by Abimelech. Call it year   (<u>2891</u>–2894)   1109
       2891

Judges 10:1–2: *"And after Abimelech there arose to defend Israel Tola the son of Puah, the son of Dodo, a man of Issachar; and he dwelt in Shamir in mount Ephraim. And he judged Israel twenty and three years, and died, and was buried in Shamir."*

104.   23 years under Tola of Issachar   <u>2894</u>–2917   1106

106.   Eli born   2912   1088

Judges 10:3: *"And after him arose Jair, a Gileadite, and judged Israel twenty and two years."*

107.   22 years under Jair, a Gileadite.   <u>2917</u>–2939   1083

Judges 10:6–8:

And the children of Israel did evil again in the sight of the LORD, and served Baalim and Ashtaroth, and the gods of Syria, and the gods of Zidon, and the gods of Moab, and the gods of the children of Ammon, and the gods of the Philistines, and forsook the LORD, and served not him. And the anger of the LORD was hot against Israel, and he sold them into the hands of the Philistines, and into the hands of the children of Ammon. And that year they vexed and op-pressed the children of Israel: eighteen years, all the children of Israel that were on the other side Jordan in the land of the Amorites, which is in Gilead.

These eighteen years of vexation and oppression by the Ammonites related to *"the children of Israel that were on the other side Jordan in the land of the Amorites, which is in Gilead."* It is fitting that Jephthah of Gilead judged and was the instrument of deliverance and in the last eighteen years of Jair's judgeship over Israel.

108.	18 years' oppression by Ammonites	(2921–2939)	1079

Judges 12:7: *"And Jephthah judged Israel six years. Then died Jephthah the Gileadite, and was buried in one of the cities of Gilead."*

109.	6 years under Jephthah, the Gileadite	2939–2945	1061

Judges 12:8–9: *"And after him Ibzan of Bethlehem judged Israel. And he had thirty sons, and thirty daughters, whom he sent abroad, and took in thirty daughters from abroad for his sons. And he judged Israel seven years."*

110.	7 years under Ibzan of Bethlehem	2945–2952	1055

Judges 12:11: *"And after him Elon, a Zebulonite, judged Israel; and he judged Israel ten years."*

111.	10 years under Eglon, a Zebulonite	2952–2962	1048

Judges 12:13–14: *"And after him Abdon the son of Hillel, a Pirathonite, judged Israel. And he had forty sons and thirty nephews, that rode on threescore and ten ass colts: and he judged Israel eight years."*

112.	8 years under Abdon, a Pirathonite	2962–2970	1038

Judges 13:1–2, 24; 15:20: *"And the children of Israel did evil again in the sight of the LORD; and the LORD delivered them into the hand of the Philistines forty years. And there was a certain man of Zorah, of the family of the Danites, whose name was Manoah; and his wife was barren, and bare not... And the woman bare a son, and called his name Samson: and the child grew, and the LORD blessed him... And he judged Israel in the days of the Philistines twenty years."*

113.	40 years delivered into hands of Philistines	2970–3010	1030

Samson judged Israel, at least in part, twenty years during the forty-year Philistine dominion over Israel. The exact years relative to that forty years we do not know.

Regarding Saul becoming king in the year of man 2984: Saul's choice as king was not God's perfect will but rather a result of the cries and demands of the people. His reign was marked with disobedience and sin. The beginning of Saul's reign did not mark the end of the effective forty-year oppression by Israel's enemies, the Philistines and the Ammonites. That deliverance came twenty-six years into Saul's forty-year rule (2984 to 3010=26).

First Samuel 4:15, 18: *"Now Eli was ninety and eight years old; and his eyes were dim, that he could not see. And it came to pass, when he made mention of the ark of God, that he fell from off the seat backward by the side of the gate, and his neck brake, and he died: for he was an old man, and heavy. And he had judged Israel forty years."*

Calculating the beginning of Eli's forty years' judgeship: The ark was absent twenty years and ten months (twenty-one years), and that absence began at the same time Eli died. As mentioned in verse 18 above, it was the taking of the ark that marked Eli's death. The twenty years and ten months' absence of the ark is determined thus: The ark was *"in the country of the Philistines seven months"* (2 Sam. 6:1). *"And it came to pass, while the ark abode in Kir-jath-je-a-rim, that the time was long; for it was twenty years: and all the house of Israel lamented after the LORD"* (1 Sam. 7:2). *"And the ark of the LORD continued in the house of Obed-edom the Gittite three months"* (2 Sam. 6:11). (7 months+20 years+3 months=20 years, 10 months, or 21 years)

The Ark was returned to Jerusalem the year King David moved his throne from Hebron to Jerusalem, the year 3031. Backdate twenty-one years from 3031 to get the year of the Ark's capture and Eli's death; also the year of the beginning of the *"days"* of Samuel and the Philistines' decisive defeat, ending forty years of Philistine domination. That would be the year 3010 (3031-21=3010). Recounting: Philistine's dominion of forty years, 2970 to 3010.

Regarding Eli's birth and death: As determined, Eli died in the year 3010. Subtracting his lifespan of ninety-eight years from the year of his death, we arrive at 2912 as the year of Eli's birth (3010-98=2912). If Eli's forty years' judgeship ended when he died, then his judgeship began in 2970 (2912+58=2970) when he was fifty-eight years of age (98-40=58). While it is conjecture, more likely, Eli's effectual judgeship began earlier and ended years before his death. That would mean that Samuel was the acting counsel during the last years of Eli's life. An overriding consideration is that Samuel was that transition person from judge to prophet. Samuel was God's instrument in orchestrating Saul's kingship in the year 2984. That would have been twenty-six years before Eli died (2984 to 3010=26). Samuel died in the timeframe of Saul's defeat and death, approximating the year 3024. Samuel's sole judgeship would have been from Eli's death in 3010, onward to the year of his and Saul's death in the year 3024—a span of fourteen years (3010 to 3024=14).

114.	40 years under Eli	<u>2970</u>–3010	1030
115.	Saul begins 40-year reign as king; Beginning of Kings' Dominion	2984	1016

Refreshing the point: Explicit dates of Samuel's judgeship are not given. In the overview of the chronological chart of years, it seems to be a non-factor. However, treating the chronology more carefully, there is the need to know the time of beginning *"all the days of Samuel."* The reason being: That "beginning" marks the end of forty years of Philistine domination.

We do know from the text in 1 Samuel that Eli's death was coincidental with the taking of the Ark. We know twenty-one years expired before the Ark was introduced into the Jerusalem location. That event was in the year 3031 when David began to reign in Jerusalem. Backdating twenty-one years, we have the year of Eli's death 3010 (3031-21=3010). The end of the forty years of Philistine rule will be thus dated as 3010. The beginning of the forty-year Philistine rule would be 2970 (3010-40=2970).

Regarding the end of that forty-year Philistine dominion: God wrought a great and decisive victory over the Philistines. According to the narrative beginning in 1 Samuel 7, the victory and Samuel's "days" were about twenty-one years before the Ark's return and within the year of Eli's death, the year 3010.

1 Sam. 7:12–13: *"Then Samuel took a stone, and set it between Mizpeh and Shen, and called the name of it Eben-ezer, saying, 'Hitherto hath the LORD helped us.' So the Philistines were subdued, and they came no more into the coast of Israel: and the hand of the LORD was against the Philistines all the days of Samuel."*

1 Samuel 4:18: *"And he (Eli) died: for he was an old man, and heavy. And he had judged Israel forty years."*

117.	Philistines take the Ark of God;	3010	990
	Eli died @ 98;		
	Decisive Philistine defeat ending 40 years' domination		

1 Samuel 7:2–3, 11–13:

And it came to pass, while the ark abode in Kirjath-jearim, that the time was long; for it was twenty years: and all the house of Israel lamented after the LORD. And Samuel spake unto all the house of Israel, saying, If ye do return unto the LORD with all your hearts, then put away the strange gods and Ashtaroth from among you, and prepare your hearts unto the LORD, and serve him only: and he will deliver you out of the hand of the Philistines... And the men of Israel went out of Mizpeh, and pursued the Philistines, and smote them, until they came under Beth-car. Then Samuel took a stone, and set it between Mizpeh and Shen, and called the name of it Eben-ezer, saying, Hitherto hath the LORD helped us. So the Philistines were subdued, and they came no more into the coast of Israel: and the hand of the LORD was against the Philistines all the days of Samuel.

Acts 13:20 states, *"And after that he gave unto them judges about the space of four hundred and fifty years, until Samuel the prophet."* Thus, we use the death of Eli and beginning of the sole administration of Samuel as the end of the time of the judges. Figuring from the beginning of Othniel's rest, the time of the judges would be 296 years (2714 to 3010). Figuring from the beginning as the death of Joshua and lifting up of Cushan in 2739 to 2747, the time of the judges would be 263 to 271 years. (The apostle Paul's mention of 450 years, as per this statement, is not deciphered as to the start or ending.)

1 Samuel 7:15: *"And Samuel judged Israel all the days of his life."*

118.	Samuel died	estimate	3024	976

TIMES PROPHESIED

69.	Jacob and family to Egypt ··································	2238	1762
70.	Begin 430-year period		
78.	Moses born ···	2588	1412
	Begin 480 years of 1 Kings 6:1		

430 years

(80+400=480) 80 years

84.	Exodus event···	2668	1332
	End of 430-year sojourn period		
117.	Ark captured, beginning 21 years ··············	3010	990
	absence; Eli died		

(400+80=480) 400 years

21 years

121.	David begins 33-year reign in Jerusalem; ··········	3031	969
	After 21 years, the ark returned		

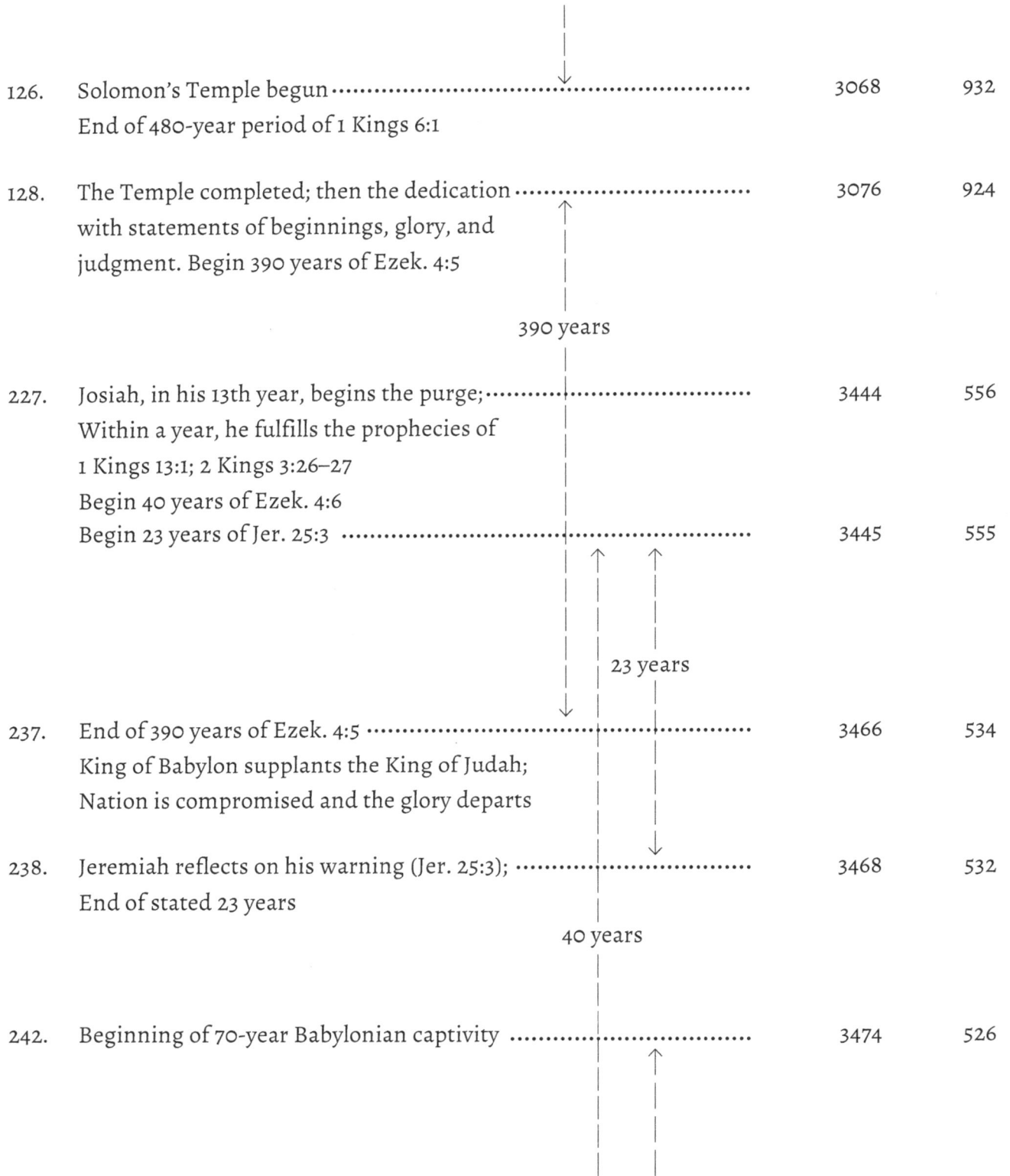

126.	Solomon's Temple begun ···································· End of 480-year period of 1 Kings 6:1	3068	932
128.	The Temple completed; then the dedication ·············· with statements of beginnings, glory, and judgment. Begin 390 years of Ezek. 4:5	3076	924

390 years

227.	Josiah, in his 13th year, begins the purge; ··········· Within a year, he fulfills the prophecies of 1 Kings 13:1; 2 Kings 3:26–27 Begin 40 years of Ezek. 4:6 Begin 23 years of Jer. 25:3 ·························	3444 3445	556 555

23 years

237.	End of 390 years of Ezek. 4:5 ····················· King of Babylon supplants the King of Judah; Nation is compromised and the glory departs	3466	534
238.	Jeremiah reflects on his warning (Jer. 25:3); ········· End of stated 23 years	3468	532

40 years

242.	Beginning of 70-year Babylonian captivity ···········	3474	526

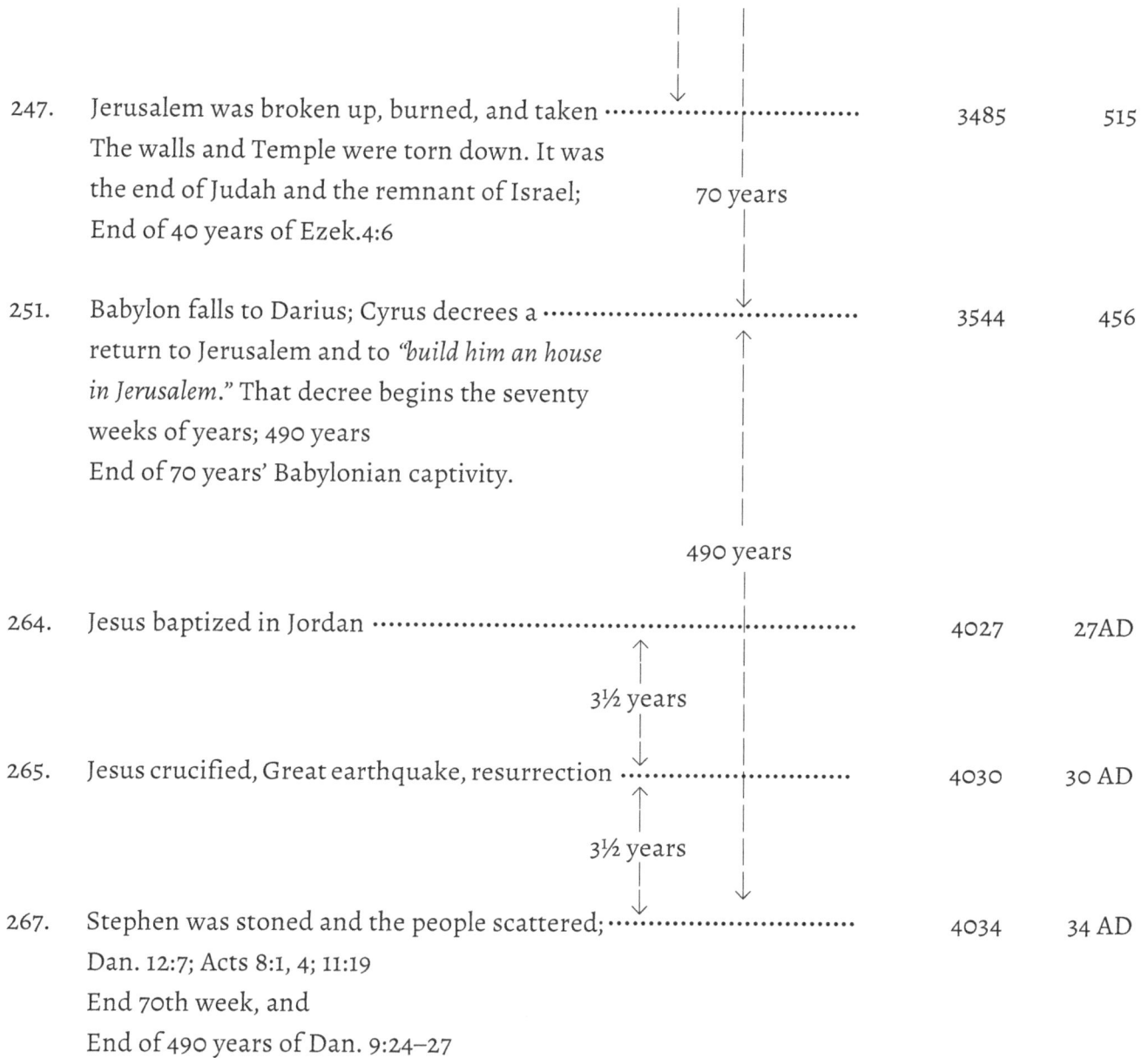

247. Jerusalem was broken up, burned, and taken   3485   515
      The walls and Temple were torn down. It was
      the end of Judah and the remnant of Israel;
      End of 40 years of Ezek.4:6

      70 years

251. Babylon falls to Darius; Cyrus decrees a   3544   456
      return to Jerusalem and to *"build him an house
      in Jerusalem."* That decree begins the seventy
      weeks of years; 490 years
      End of 70 years' Babylonian captivity.

      490 years

264. Jesus baptized in Jordan   4027   27AD

      3½ years

265. Jesus crucified, Great earthquake, resurrection   4030   30 AD

      3½ years

267. Stephen was stoned and the people scattered;   4034   34 AD
      Dan. 12:7; Acts 8:1, 4; 11:19
      End 70th week, and
      End of 490 years of Dan. 9:24–27

CHAPTER 6

CONCEPTS OF A SUBJECTIVE KIND

IT IS A BENEFIT to the reader, enhancing the reading, if perchance fresh and insightful, precepts would catapult "old data" into the column of "present truth."

These items are insightful, even pertinent, and encouraging toward the study of God's timing. While meaningful, they do not affect the chronology. There is limited integrating into the "Reference Addendum," where the depictions and explanations appear. Dedicated charts are shown in order of the presentation.

Six Eras

This 4000-year period of this chronological study can be divided into six divisions of 666.6 years. Interestingly, the lifetime of known icons of faith and one specified dispensation over span the time breaks, thus denoting the period breaks. An encouragement to introduce this precept was the connected scripture: Hebrews 11:4–5, 7–8, 23, 32.

> By faith **Abel** offered unto God a more excellent sacrifice than Cain, by which he obtained witness that he was righteous, God testifying of his gifts: and by it he being dead yet speaketh. By faith **Enoch** was translated that he should not see death; and was not found, because God had translated him: for before his translation he had this testimony, that he pleased God... By faith **Noah**, being warned of God of things not seen as yet, moved with fear, prepared an ark to the saving of his house; by the which he condemned the world, and became heir of the righteousness which is by faith. By faith **Abraham**, when he was called to go out into a place which he should after receive for an inheritance, obeyed; and he went... By faith **Moses**, when he was born, was hid three months of his parents, because they saw he was a proper child; and they were not afraid of the king's commandment... And what shall I more say? For the time would fail me to tell of Gideon, and of Barak, and of Samson, and of Jephthae; of David **(Kings)** also, and Samuel, and of the prophets: **Jesus** was the seventh, fulfilling all righteousness.

Chart Denoting Six Eras

BEGIN FIRST ERA			0	4000
3.	**Abel;** his offering and death established a righteous line		unknown	
9.	**Enoch** born		622	3378
BEGIN SECOND ERA		666	666	3334
13.	**Enoch** died		987	3013
15.	**Noah** born		1056	2944
BEGIN THIRD ERA		1333	1333	2667
37.	**Noah** died		2006	1992
33.	**Abram** born		1948	2052
BEGIN FORTH ERA		2000	2000	2000
55.	**Abraham** died		2123	1877
78.	**Moses** born		2588	1412
BEGIN FIFTH ERA		2667	2667	1333
89.	**Moses** died		2708	1292
120.	**King David** begins reign.		3024	976
BEGIN SIXTH ERA		3333	3333	667
233.	**King Josiah** died		3463	537
263.	**Jesus** born		3996	4 BC
END SIXTH ERA				
BEGIN SEVENTH ERA		4000	4000	0
Jesus died and established the righteous line of Christ			4030	30 AD

Chart of Interest

(Treating the Idea of a No Time Reckoning)

The report of Gen. 6:5–8:19, regarding the flood in Noah's time, relates the prolonged precipitation, the coincidental atmospheric collapse, and a breaking up of the underground aquifers. The results are first, a slight increase of the earth's rate of rotation on its axis. Second, it significantly decreased atmospheric pressure. With the reduced atmospheric pressure, all animal life would experience a reduction of oxygen in the blood, thus the introduction of root health issues, also a decrease of atmospheric protection from the sun's damaging radiation. Third, the ratio of water to land was increased to approximately 71 percent water and approximately 29 percent land. These phenomena are more than mere supposition. Further astronomical and physical factors could be treated and reported. The downside of the argument here is that scientific contests may become cumbersome and counterproductive—certainly beyond the scope of this writing. Hopefully, this very abbreviated report will be given consideration, at least entertained, and at best accepted.

What needs to enter the narrative is the particular point having to do with the earth's rotation. Herein lies the basis of the proposition of a 360-day year before the flood and the 365-¼-day year after the flood. (From a quantitative standpoint, it is questionable if the atmospheric collapse alone would cause such a magnitude of change. Other phenomena were likely in play.)

Regarding a future restoration: The atmosphere will be restored and again provide sufficient protection from the sun's damaging radiation and more favorable blood oxygen levels. All health issues will pass. The ratio of water surface to earth surface will again favor the earth. The aquifers that broke through the earth will be restored. Mankind will again enjoy a 360-day year with a thirty-day lunar cycle.

The heartbeat of the discussion: It is more than coincidental that the added 5¼ days per year, dating from the flood and then forward to Christ, equals the life span of Christ. (4,000-1,656=2,344) (2,344x5¼=12,306) (12,306/365¼=33.7) The 33.7 years approximates 33 years 8 months.

If God's intent was to zero the clock, in terms of the original, then so be it. Assuredly, the flood was God's statement toward sin, and Christ's sinless life is God's statement toward the redemption of all things. Man's days are numbered because of sin, and Christ's days were not numbered, he being without sin.

For the purpose of demonstrating the point, we will use the structure of the Chart Denoting Six Eras. As shown, the 4000-year period of this chronological study can be divided into six divisions of 666.6 years. Relating to this Chart of Interest, we take the occasion to insert the corrected years in bold type. That is, calculated with respect to a 360-day year versus a 365¼-day year. This chart of interest incorporates this time correction feature as a "non-time-reckoning" of Christ's 33½ years' sinless life; call it 34 years. That would be thirty years if reckoning the time correction as between

Christ's birth and forward to his baptism in Jordan, the time of his innocence. He was without sin for 33½ years, but he did carry the sins of mankind for the last 3½ years of his life. As it was in the culmination on the cross, *"For he hath made him to be sin for us, who knew no sin; that we might be made the righteousness of God in him"* (2 Cor. 5:21). Likewise, Adam's pre-fall time of a self-determined, sinless life might be given the same thirty years, "non-time-reckoning." Jesus is the *"second man"* (1 Cor. 15:47). That would be the Christ-Adam similitude. Whereas Adam failed his trial of faith, Jesus, at age thirty, did not. The somewhat-hidden point here is that the numbering of days is essentially a countdown to an end. An end of life in terms of "thou shalt surely die." A "sin" factor. This is a mystery, and regarding this Chart of Interest, it is mentioned because it is the basis of the precept.

Repeating the premises: The time of Adam's innocence and self-determination is unstated. However speculative, there is the possibility Adam lived thirty years before he sinned. Considering the time-consuming task of naming the animals and the record of life events, the allotment of thirty years is not unreasonable. The basis for this venture is the similitude of Christ having lived thirty years before being tempted by the devil.

This thirty-year conjecture is not a time-reckoned addition to Adam's 930-year lifetime. Thus, the chronology is unaffected. The conjecture, in total, is not a part of the chronology.

Chart of Interest

	Time of Man		Date BC
Adam created and given life with no time reckoning		o	o
BEGIN FIRST ERA– 1st heaven, 1st earth:		o	4000
Adam's fall; sin enters			
BEGIN SECOND ERA	666	666	3334
BEGIN THIRD ERA	1333	1333	2667
FLOOD		1656	2344
BEGIN FORTH ERA	2000	2000	2000

Corrected as per 360 vs. 365¼ day year: 2000=**2005**

BEGIN FIFTH ERA	2667	2667	1333

Corrected as per 360 vs. 365¼ day year: 2667=**2682**

BEGIN SIXTH ERA	3333	3333	667

Corrected as per 360 vs. 365¼ day year: 3333=**3357**

JESUS BORN		3996	4

END SIXTH ERA

BEGIN SEVENTH ERA	4000	4000	o

Corrected as per 360 vs. 365¼ day year: 4000=**4030**

TO WIT:

JESUS BORN	3996	4

Corrected as per 360 vs. 365¼ day year: 3996=**4030**

The time of Christ's innocence, totaling 34 years, is not reckoned: So that, from the year of his birth, 3996, till his death, 4030, is not reckoned. That brings the "adjusted" year of his birth, **4030,** to a unity with the year of his crucifixion, which is 4030.

Jesus crucified	4030	30 AD

CHAPTER 7

CHRONOLOGY; THE REFERENCE ADDENDUM

THE KING JAMES VERSION is used throughout with emphasis added. Scripture is given in italics with underlining. Additions to the text are in parentheses and not italicized.

Scripture substantiating the dates precede the item number of the date of interest. Related statements follow the item of interest. So that the reporting of years does not encumber the page, unless otherwise noted, dates are understood to be in years. Most dates lack the inclusion of months and days. As such, the year given may slide one year back or one year forward.

"Era" inclusions leave the chronology unaffected.

1. *"In the beginning God created the heaven and the earth."* Gen. 1:1

	(Anno Hominis) Time of Man Date	BC
BEGIN FIRST ERA	0	4000
2. *Adam	0	4000
3. Abel born of Adam	unknown	

Gen. 5:3–5: *"And Adam lived an <u>hundred and thirty years</u>, and begat a son... And the days of Adam after he had begotten Seth were <u>eight hundred years</u>: And all the days that Adam lived were <u>nine hundred and thirty years</u>: and he died."*

4.   *Seth born of Adam @ 130   130   3870

130-0=130, age of Adam at son's birth

Gen. 5:6–8: "And Seth lived an _hundred and five years_, and begat Enos: And Seth lived after he begat Enos _eight hundred and seven years_, ... And all the days of Seth were _nine hundred and twelve years_: and he died."

5.   *Enos born of Seth @ 105   235   3765

235-130=105, age of Seth at son's birth

Gen. 5:9–11. "And Enos lived _ninety years_, and begat Cainan: And Enos lived after he begat Cainan eight hundred and fifteen years, ...And all the days of Enos were _nine hundred and five years_: and he died."

6.   *Cainan born of Enos @ 90   325   3675

325-235=90, age of Enos at son's birth

Gen. 5:12–14: "And Cainan lived _seventy years_, and begat Mahalaleel: And Cainan lived after he begat Mahalaleel _eight hundred and forty years_, ... And all the days of Cainan were _nine hundred and ten years_: and he died."

7.   *Mahalaleel born of Cainan @ 70   395   3605

395-325=70, age of Cainan at son's birth

Gen. 5:15–17: "And Mahalaleel lived _sixty and five years_, and begat Jared: And Mahalaleel lived after he begat Jared _eight hundred and thirty years_, ... And all the days of Mahalaleel were _eight hundred ninety and five years_ and he died."

8.   *Jared born of Mahalaleel @ 65   460   3540

460-395=65, age of Mahalaleel at son's birth

Gen. 5:18–20: "And Jared lived an _hundred sixty and two years_, and he begat Enoch: And Jared lived after he begat Enoch _eight hundred years_, ... And all the days of Jared were _nine hundred sixty and two years_: and he died."

9.   *Enoch born of Jared @ 162   622   3378

622-460=162, age of Jared at son's birth

BEGIN SECOND ERA   666   666   3334

Gen. 5:21–23: "And Enoch lived _sixty and five years_, and begat Methuselah: And Enoch walked with God after he begat Methuselah _three hundred years_, ... And all the days of Enoch were _three hundred sixty and five years_:"

| 10. | *Methuselah born of Enoch @ 65 | | 687 | 3313 |
| | 687-622=65, age of Enoch at son's birth | | | |

Gen. 5:25–27: "And Methuselah lived an _hundred eighty and seven years_, and begat Lamech. And Methuselah lived after he begat Lamech _seven hundred eighty and two years_, ... And all the days of Methuselah were _nine hundred sixty and nine years_: and he died."

11.	*Lamech born of Methuselah @ 187		874	3126
	874-687=187, age of Methuselah at his birth			
12.	Adam died @ 930		930	3070
13.	Enoch died @ 365		987	3013
14.	Seth died @ 912		1042	2958

Gen. 5:28–31: "And Lamech lived an _hundred eighty and two years_, and begat a son: And he called his name Noah, ... And Lamech lived after he begat Noah _five hundred ninety and five years_, ... And all the days of Lamech were _seven hundred seventy and seven years_: and he died."

15.	*Noah born of Lamech @ 182		1056	2944
	1056-874=182, age of Lamech at son's birth			
16.	Enos died @ 905		1140	2860
17.	Cainan died @ 910		1235	2765
18.	Mahalaleel died @ 895		1290	2710
14.	Seth died @ 912		1042	2958
BEGIN THIRD ERA		1333	1333	2667
19.	Jared died @ 962		1422	2578

Gen. 5:32: "And Noah was _five hundred years old_: and Noah begat Shem, Ham, and Japheth."

20. *Shem born of Noah @ 500   1556   2444
    1556-1056=500, age of Noah at son's birth

21. Lamech died @ 777   1651   2349

22. Methuselah died @ 969   1656   2344

Gen. 7:6: "*And Noah was six hundred years old when the flood of waters was upon the earth.*"

Gen. 9:28–29: "*And Noah lived after the flood three hundred and fifty years. And all the years of Noah were nine hundred and fifty years: and he died.*"

23. FLOOD   1656   2344

Gen. 11:10–11: "*These are the generations of Shem: Shem was an hundred years old, and begat Arphaxad two years after the flood: And Shem lived after he begat Arphaxad five hundred years...*"

(That would make Seth 600 years old at the time of his death. It is understood that "*an hundred years old*" mentioned in verse 10 refers to the age of Shem at the time of the flood.)

24. *Arphaxad born of Shem @ 102   1658   2342
    1658-1556=102, age of Shem at son's birth

Gen.11:12–13: "*And Arphaxad lived five and thirty years, and begat Salah: 13. And Arphaxad lived after he begat Salah four hundred and three years...*"

(That would make Arphaxad 438 years old at the time of his death.)

25. *Salah born of Arphaxad @ 35   1693   2307
    1693-1658=35, age of Arphaxad at son's birth

Gen. 11:14–15: "*And Salah lived thirty years, and begat Eber: And Salah lived after he begat Eber four hundred and three years...*"

(That would make Salah 433 years old at the time of his death.)

26. *Eber born of Salah @ 30   1723   2277
    1723-1693=30, age of Salah at son's birth

Gen. 11:16–17: "*And Eber lived four and thirty years, and begat Peleg: And Eber lived after he begat Peleg four hundred and thirty years...*"

(That would make Eber 464 years old at the time of his death.)

27.   *Peleg born of Eber @ 34   1757   2243
        1757-1723=34, age of Eber at son's birth

        Gen. 11:18–19: *"And Peleg lived <u>thirty years</u>, and begat Reu: And Peleg lived after he begat Reu <u>two hundred and nine years</u>..."*
        (That would make Peleg 239 years old at the time of his death.)

28.   *Reu born of Peleg @ 30   1787   2213
        1787-1757=30, age of Peleg at son's birth

        Gen. 10:25: *"And unto Eber were born two sons: the name of one was Peleg; for in his days was the earth divided."*
        Regarding this statement of "divided" associated with the tower of Babel and the confusion of language: Peleg's lifespan was 1757–1996. The division likely occurred after Reu was born, in 1787, and before Reu's first child, Serug, in 1819; call it 1817.

29.   The Tower of Babel-Confusion   approximation   1817   2183

        Gen. 11:20–21: *"And Reu lived <u>two and thirty years</u>, and begat Serug: And Reu lived after he begat Serug <u>two hundred and seven years</u>..."*
        (That would make Reu 239 years old at the time of his death.)

30.   *Serug born of Reu @ 32   1819   2181
        1819-1787=32, age of Reu at son's birth

        Gen. 11:22–23: *"And Serug lived <u>thirty years</u>, and begat Nahor: And Serug lived after he begat Nahor <u>two hundred years</u>..."*
        (That would make Serug 230 years old at the time of his death.)

31.   *Nahor born of Serug @ 30   1849   2151
        1849-1819=30, age of Serug at son's birth

        Gen. 11:24–25: *"And Nahor lived <u>nine and twenty years</u>, and begat Terah: And Nahor lived after he begat Terah an <u>hundred and nineteen years</u>..."*
        (That would make Nahor 148 years old at the time of his death.)

32.   *Terah born of Nahor @ 29   1878   2122
        1878-1849=29, age of Nahor at son's birth

Gen. 11:26, 32: *"And Terah lived seventy years, and begat Abraham, Nahor, and Haran. And the days of Terah were two hundred and five years: and Terah died in Haran."*

(That would make Terah 275 years old at the time of his death.)

33.	*Abram born of Terah @ 70	1948	2052
	1948-1878=70, age of Terah at son's birth		

Gen. 17:17: *"Then Abraham fell upon his face, and laughed, and said in his heart, Shall a child be born unto him that is an hundred years old? And shall Sarah, that is ninety years old bear?"*

(Abraham was born in 1948 and Sarah, being ten years younger, would have been born in 1958.) Gen. 23:1: *"And Sarah was an hundred and seven and twenty years old: these were the years of the life of Sarah."*

34.	Sarai born	1958	2042
35.	Peleg died @ 239	1996	2004
36.	Nahor died @ 148	1997	2003

BEGIN FORTH ERA		2000	2000	2000
37.	Noah died @ 950		2006	1994
38.	Abraham and family to Canaan		2023	1977

Gen. 12:1, 4: *"Now the Lord had said unto Abram, Get thee out of thy country, and from thy kindred, and from thy father's house, unto a land that I will shew thee: So Abram departed, as the Lord had spoken unto him; and Lot went with him: and Abram was seventy and five years old when he departed out of Haran."*

The above scripture, with Gen. 11:26 given earlier, conflict with Acts 7:4, where Stephen states in Acts 7:4, *"Then came he (Abram) out of the land of the Chaldaeans, and dwelt in Charran: and from thence, when his father was dead, he removed him into this land, wherein ye now dwell."* Considering first that *"and from thy father's house"* in Gen. 12:1, infers that Terah was alive when Abram left Haran. Secondly, Gen. 11:26 states, *"And Terah lived seventy years, and begat Abram, Nahor, and Haran."* On this last point, it is reasonable that while Abram was not the oldest, he was mentioned first, so that the chronological statement of seventy should apply to Abraham's birth and not Haran. Acts 7:4 is a different account from the idea that Abraham left Haran before his father died. This chronology gives preference to the Old Testament account.

39.	Reu died @ 239	2026	1974
40.	Abram @ 85 married Hagar	2033	1967

Gen. 16:15–16: *"And Hagar bare Abram a son: and Abram called his son's name, which Hagar bare, Ishmael. And Abram was fourscore and six years old, when Hagar bare Ishmael to Abram."*

41.	Ishmael born to Abram @ 86	2034	1966
42.	Covenant of circumcision; Abram renamed Abraham	2047	1953
43.	Isaac promised; Sarai renamed Sarah	2047	1953

Gen. 17:1–15, 19:

And when Abram was <u>ninety years old and nine</u>, the LORD appeared to Abram, and said unto him, I [am] the Almighty God; walk before me, and be thou perfect. And I will make my covenant between me and thee, and will multiply thee exceedingly. And Abram fell on his face: and God talked with him, saying, As for me, behold, my covenant [is] with thee, and thou shalt be a father of many nations. Neither shall thy name any more be called Abram, but thy name shall be Abraham; for a father of many nations have I made thee. And I will make thee exceeding fruitful, and I will make nations of thee, and kings shall come out of thee. And I will establish my covenant between me and thee and thy seed after thee in their generations for an everlasting covenant, to be a God unto thee, and to thy seed after thee. And I will give unto thee, and to thy seed after thee, the land wherein thou art a stranger, all the land of Canaan, for an everlasting possession; and I will be their God. And God said unto Abraham, Thou shalt keep my covenant therefore, thou, and thy seed after thee in their generations. This is my covenant, which ye shall keep, between me and you and thy seed after thee; Every man child among you shall be circumcised. And ye shall circumcise the flesh of your foreskin; and it shall be a token of the covenant betwixt me and you. And he that is eight days old shall be circumcised among you, every man child in your generations, he that is born in the house, or bought with money of any stranger, which is not of thy seed. He that is born in thy house, and he that is bought with thy money, must needs be circumcised: and my covenant shall be in your flesh for an everlasting covenant. And the uncircumcised man child whose flesh of his foreskin is not circumcised, that soul shall be cut off from his people; he hath broken my covenant. And God said unto Abraham, As for Sarai thy wife, thou shalt not call her name Sarai, but Sarah shall her name be.... And God said, Sarah *thy wife shall bear thee a son indeed; and thou shalt call his name Isaac: and I will establish my covenant with him for an everlasting covenant, and with his seed after him.*

Gen. 17:23–25: *"And Abraham took Ishmael his son, and all that were born in his house, and all that were bought with his money, every male among the men of Abraham's house; and circumcised the flesh of their foreskin in the selfsame day, as God had said unto him. And Abraham was <u>ninety years old and nine</u>, when he was circumcised in the flesh of his foreskin. And Ishmael his son was <u>thirteen years</u> old, when he was circumcised in the flesh of his foreskin."*

44.	Circumcision: Abraham @ 99, Ishmael @ 13		2047	1953
45.	Sodom destroyed		2047	1953

Gen. 21:1–5: *"And the Lord visited Sarah as he had said, and the Lord did unto Sarah as he had spoken. For Sarah conceived, and bare Abraham a son in his old age, at the set time of which God had spoken to him. And Abraham called the name of his son that was born unto him, whom Sarah bare to him, Isaac. And Abraham circumcised his son Isaac being eight days old, as God had commanded him. And Abraham was <u>an hundred years old</u>, when his son Isaac was born unto him."*

Gen. 25:7: *"And these are the days of the years of Abraham's life which he lived, <u>an hundred threescore and fifteen years</u>."*

46.	*Isaac born of Abraham @ 100 2048-1948=100, age of Abraham at son's birth		2048	1952
47.	Serug died @ 230		2049	1951
48.	Ishmael cast out @ 20 Time frame of Isaac's weaning at age 3 to 9; call it 6.	approximation	2054	1946

Gen. 22:1–2: *"And it came to pass after these things, that God did tempt Abraham, and said unto him, Abraham: and he said, Behold, here I am. And he said, Take now thy son, thine only son Isaac, whom thou lovest, and get thee into the land of Moriah; and offer him there for a burnt offering upon one of the mountains which I will tell thee of."*

The likely age of Isaac was 30–33½ years at the time of his being offered. This is conjecture because of the absence of explicit scripture. However, Isaac was a picture of Christ offering his life and the *"ram caught in a thicket by the horns"* (Gen. 22:13), was a type of law. As said Gal. 3:19, *"It was added because of transgressions, till the seed should come to whom the promise was made; and it was ordained by angels in the hand of a mediator"* (the mediator being Moses). The reference to Isaac as a *"lad"* does not discount his age. Benjamin was referred to as a *"lad"* in Gen. 44:22–34, and he was a man with a family of possibly ten children.

49.	Isaac offered @ 30	2078	1922
50.	Terah died @ 205	2083	1917

It is a reasonable conjecture that at the time of Terah's death (Abraham's father) that the facts of Gen. 22:20–24 were *"told Abraham,"* which included mention of Rebekah; two years later, Sarah died, and three years hence, Isaac and Rebecca were married. This kind of sharing and the resulting connections would be probable with a death event.

Gen. 23:1: *"And Sarah was <u>an hundred and seven and twenty years</u> old: these were the years of the life of Sarah."*

51.	Sarah died @ 127	2085	1915

Gen. 25:20: *"And Isaac was <u>forty years old</u> when he took Rebekah to wife, the daughter of Bethuel the Syrian of Padan-aram, the sister to Laban the Syrian."*

52.	Isaac @ 40 married Rebekah	2088	1912
53.	Arphaxad died @ 438	2096	1904

Gen. 25:26–27: *"...and Isaac was <u>threescore years old</u> when she bare them. And the boys grew: and Esau was a cunning hunter, a man of the field; and Jacob was a plain man, dwelling in tents."*

54.	*Jacob and Esau born of Isaac @ 60	2108	1892
	2108-2048=60, age of Isaac at son's birth		
55.	Abraham died @ 175; Isaac @ 75	2123	1877
56.	Salah died @ 433	2126	1874

Gen. 26:34: *"And Esau was <u>forty years old</u> when he took to wife Judith the daughter of Beeri the Hittite, and Bashemath the daughter of Elon the Hittite."*

57.	Esau @ 40 married Hittite women	2148	1852
58.	Shem died @ 600	2156	1844

Gen. 25:24–28:5 relates the tale of dreadful deceit and fear. Rebekah orchestrates the deception that gains Isaac's blessing for Jacob, thus supplanting Esau. Sometime later, Jacob's life is threatened by Esau. Rebekah plans and carries out Jacob's flight to Padan-aram.

Determining Jacob's approximate age at the time he fled from Esau to Padan-aram: If we estimate the time of the birthing of eleven children by four wives, as per the Bible narrative, to be twenty-two years, then the total time in Padan-aram would be 7+22+6=35 years. The reasoning being Gen. 31:41 states, *"Thus have I been twenty years in thy house; I served thee fourteen years for thy two daughters, and six years for thy cattle: and thou hast changed my wages ten times."* The terminology *"in thy house"* can justly be saying "under thy stewardship." Laban was obviously legalistic, and the *"fourteen years for the two daughters, and six years for thy cattle,"* was referring to the years "under contract." There was at least a one-month time lapse between Jacob's arrival and the beginning of the "contract" (Gen. 29:14). There was an additional unstated space of time after fulfilling the fourteen years' contract and resetting Laban's oversight for the additional six years. The narrative of Gen. 29:31–30:24 relates the births of Jacob's eleven sons and one daughter. This could not have been accomplished in seven years. It is more likely, while unstated that the account of the births reasonably covered a time of twenty-one to twenty-two years as previously stated. Jacob was born in 2108, as per the chronology. Jacob was ninety-one years old when Joseph was born, and that was six years before the departure from Laban's stewardship. Therefore, Jacob was ninety-one years plus six years, or ninety-seven years old when he fled from Laban. That would be the year 2205 (2108+97=2205). The approximate year of the flight from Esau was 2170 (2205-35=2170). Jacob was born in 2108, so his age at the time of his flight to Padan-aram was sixty-two years (2170–2108=62).

59.	Jacob @ approx. 62 fled toward Padan-aram	estimate	2170	1830
	First blessing of God at Bethel;			
	Within the year, Jacob comes to Laban's			
	household			

Gen. 29:20–23, 28: *"And Jacob served seven years for Rachel; and they seemed unto him but a few days, for the love he had to her. And Jacob said unto Laban, Give me my wife, for my days are fulfilled, that I may go in unto her. And Laban gathered together all the men of the place, and made a feast. And it came to pass in the evening, that he took Leah his daughter, and brought her to him; and he went in unto her....and he gave him Rachel his daughter to wife also.*

| 60. | Jacob @ approx. 69 married Leah and Rachel | estimate | 2177 | 1823 |

The birth dates of the righteous line of Christ from Judah to Jessie are not given nor can they be determined exactly. We reasonably approximate those dates; they will be noted as an "estimate."

61.	*Judah born of Jacob @ 76	estimate	2184	1816
	2184-2108=76, age of Jacob at son's birth			

62.	Eber died @ 464		2187	1813

Jacob was 130 years of age when he spoke to Pharaoh. Nine years before that, Joseph stood before Pharaoh at age thirty. Seven years of plenty plus two years of famine totals nine years. Gen. 45:6 states, *"For these two years hath the famine been in the land: and yet there are five years, in the which there shall be neither earing nor harvest."* (Calculations: 130 years-9 years=121 years being Jacob's age at the time of Joseph's promotion by Pharaoh at age thirty. Thus, 121 years-30 years=91 years as Jacob's age when Joseph was born.

63.	Joseph born of Jacob @ 91		2199	1801

Gen. 30:25 states, *"And it came to pass, when Rachel had born Joseph, that Jacob said unto Laban, Send me away, that I may go unto mine own place, and to my country."* This statement indicates that Joseph was born six years before Jacob's departure from Laban's house. The reasoning being subsequent to Joseph's birth and that statement was the agreement or contract for what turned out to be an additional six years, after which Joseph departed from Laban's stewardship. *"Thus have I been twenty years in thy house; I served thee fourteen years for thy two daughters, and six years for thy cattle: and thou hast changed my wages ten times"* (Gen. 31:41).

64.	Jacob and family fled from Laban (Gen. 31)		2205	1795

65.	Jacob dwelt in Shalem an estimated 7 years (2205–2212); He gave demand to put away idols, then on to Bethel where he experienced the second blessing. God called Jacob "Israel." Later, Rachael died in childbirth.		2212	1788

Gen. 32:28, 30: *"And he said, Thy name shall be called no more Jacob, But Israel: for as a prince hast thou power with God and with men, and hast prevailed. ...And Jacob called the name of the place Peniel: for I have seen God face to face, and my life is preserved."*

Gen. 33:18–20: *"And Jacob came to Shalem, a city of Shechem, which is in the land of Canaan, when he came from Padan-aram; and pitched his tent before the city. And he bought a parcel of a field, where he had spread his tent, at the hand of the children of Hamor, Shechem's father, for an hundred pieces of money. And he erected there an alter, and called it El-el-o-he- Israel."*

Gen. 35:1–3, 9–10:

And God said unto Jacob, Arise, go up to Bethel, and dwell there: and make there an altar unto God, that appeared unto thee when thou fleddest from the face of Esau thy brother. Then Jacob said unto his household, and to all that were with him, Put away the strange gods that are among you, and be clean, and change your garments: And let us arise, and go up to Beth-el; and I will make there an altar unto God, who answered me in the day of my distress, and was with me in the way which I went... And God Appeared unto Jacob again, when he came out of Pa-dan-aram, and blessed him. And God said unto him, Thy name is Jacob: thy name shall not be called any more Jacob, but Israel shall be thy name: and he called his name Israel.

Gen. 37:2 states, *"Joseph, being <u>seventeen years old</u>, was feeding the flock with his brethren."* (The narrative continues with detail of the brethren's irritations regarding Joseph. No space of time is given, if any, between the statement of his age and him being sold into slavery. It is reasonably considered that the statement of Joseph's age and the sale into slavery were in the same time frame.)

66.	Joseph @ 17 sold into slavery	2216	1784

Gen. 35:28: *"And the days of Isaac were <u>an hundred and fourscore years</u>. And Isaac gave up the ghost, and died, and was gathered unto his people, being old and full of days: and his sons Esau and Jacob buried him."*

67.	Isaac died @ 180	2228	1772

Gen. 41:46: *"And Joseph was <u>thirty years old</u> when he stood before Pharaoh king of Egypt."*

68.	Joseph @ 30 stood before Pharaoh	2229	1771

As per the narrative, Joseph was thirteen years in the distress of slavery before being exalted to ruler status in Egypt, seventeen years of age to thirty years of age.

Gen47:8–9: *"And Pharaoh said unto Jacob, How old art thou? And Jacob said unto Pharaoh, The days of the years of my pilgrimage are <u>an hundred and thirty years</u>..."*

69.	Jacob @ 130, and family to Egypt (Joseph @ 39)	2238	1762

Exod. 12:40–41 states, *"Now the sojourning of the children of Israel, who dwelt in Egypt, was <u>four hundred and thirty years</u>. And it came to pass <u>at the end of</u> <u>the four hundred and thirty years</u>, even <u>the selfsame day</u>, it came to pass that all the hosts of the Lord went out from the land of Egypt."*

70.	Begin 430-year period	2238	1762

Gen. 47:28: *"And Jacob lived in the land of Egypt <u>seventeen years</u>: so the whole age of Jacob was <u>an hundred forty and seven years</u>"* (130+17=147).

71.	Jacob died @ 147		2255	1745

Explicit dates for the record are continuous up to this point. Hereafter some estimated dates are included. The estimated dates are not critical to the continuity of the chronology. From this point to the time of the kings we have the "intervals" given from which we determine the continuity of the chronology. The 430 years of Exod. 12:41–42 mentioned above is the first "interval" that takes us from the Egypt-sojourn to the Exodus event.

72.	*Phares born of Judah @ +99 2283-2184=99, age of Judah at son's birth	estimate	2283	1717
73.	Joseph died @ 110		2309	1691
74.	*Esrom born of Phares @ 72 2355-2283=72, age of Phares at son's birth	estimate	2355	1645
75.	*Aram born Esrom @ 72 2427-2355=72, age of Esrom at son's birth	estimate	2427	1573
76.	*Aminadab born of Aram @ 72 2499-2427=72, age of Aram at son's birth	estimate	2499	1501
77.	*Naason born of Aminadab @ 72 2571-2499=72, age of Aminadab at son's birth	estimate	2571	1429

The date of Moses' birth is determined by dating back from the known date of the Exodus, 2668, at which time Moses was eight years old (2668-80=2588).

78.	Moses born Begin 480 years of 1 Kings 6:1		2588	1412

Determining the date of the Exodus requires that we reference the 480 years' interval given in 1 Kings 6:1: *"And it came to pass in the <u>four hundred and eightieth year</u> after the children of Israel were come out of the land of Egypt, in the <u>fourth year</u> of Solomon's reign over Israel, in the month Zif, which is the second month, that he began to build the house of the Lord."*

The reasoning given here alters the thought-to-be beginning of the 480 years' time span given in 1 Kings 6:1.

To wit: Moses' birth and the history surrounding his salvation and maturity in the house of Pharaoh are rightfully given with great detail in scripture, as was Christ's birth and time forward to his beginning of ministry. Moses was the marker of deliverance, the Exodus. God's covenant with the children of Israel, eighty years later, was subordinate to God's covenant with Moses, the apostle of God. The Exodus/deliverance and Passover were characteristic and typical of Christ. Moses was the then-present mediator. Moses represents the law, and that is a real aspect and valid consideration in the overview. This 480-year period begins at the ending of approximately 2,500 years of man's tenure without a written law. The 480 years' interval starts with Moses' birth. Again, the overriding aspect was Moses' personage. The Exodus is an eighty-year epic, and the "event" was accomplished "even the selfsame day." Following the eighty-year Exodus was the 400-year dispensation, dating from the giving of the law to the building of the Temple, the place where God's presence abode. Moses is the Old Testament apostle of God. As such, his birth was recorded with detail, as was Jesus' birth. It was the marker and beginning of the 480 years of 1 Kings 6:1. Moses was the avenue of God's deliverance of his people. Moses was God's gift, dispensed, as a steward, dispensing and authoring the Exodus. Moses' birth is the beginning mark of the Exodus, and he was, "on that very day," primary in the Exodus event itself.

In the overview, that first eighty years was the Exodus narrative. Crossing over was the Exodus event. The additional 400 years concluded the total 480-year dispensation.

Looking forward: 2588+80+400=3068 as the year of the beginning of the construction of Solomon's Temple.

Acts 7:23: "And when he was _full forty years old_, it came into his heart to visit his brethren the children of Israel."

Moses encountered rejection and the developing situation caused him to flee for his life.

Acts 7:29: "_Then fled Moses at this saying and was a stranger in the land of Madian, where he begat two sons._" 2588+40=2628

79.	Moses @ 40 fled Egypt	2628	1372

Josh. 14:7: "_Forty years old_ was I when Moses the servant of the LORD sent me from Kadesh-bar-ne-a to espy out the land:"

This was spoken concerning Caleb who was confederate with Joshua. Caleb was forty years old at the time of his dispatch to spy the land; that being the second year after the Exodus, the year 2669. Thus, his birthdate was 2629 (2669–40=2629).

80.	Caleb born	2629	1371

We have no definitive date for Joshua's birth. Reckoning that Joshua and Caleb were approximately the same age, Joshua likely the younger, we presume an estimated birth date for Joshua as the year 2629.

81.	Joshua born	estimate	2629	1371
82.	*Salmon born of Naason @ 72	estimate	2643	1357
	2643-2571=72, age of Naason at son's birth			

BEGIN FIFTH ERA	2667	2667	1333

Exod. 12:40–41 states, *"Now the sojourning of the children of Israel, who dwelt in Egypt, was <u>four hundred and thirty years</u>. And it came to pass <u>at the end of the four hundred and thirty years, even the selfsame day</u>, it came to pass that all the hosts of the Lord went out from the land of Egypt."*

Also, Gal. 3:16–17 states, *"Now to Abraham and his seed were the promises made. He saith not, And to seeds, as of many; but as of one, And to thy seed, which is Christ. And this I say, that the covenant, that was confirmed before of God in Christ, the law, which was <u>four hundred and thirty years</u> after, cannot disannul, that it should make the promise of none effect."*

Gal. 3:17 gives the 430-year end point as the giving of the law. That is correct because the event of the giving of the law was within the year of the Exodus event. Galatians mentions Abraham in particular, whose covenant was about 120 years earlier. *"And his seed"* stated above is certainly inclusive of the Abrahamic covenant. The third generation person, Jacob, has the same covenant reaffirmed twofold, both at Bethel. First, at the time of his flight, being alone, to Padan-aram. The second time, with his family (seed), experiencing his God-ordained name change to Israel. Having fled Laban's stewardship, God "called his name Israel" (Gen. 35:10).

Jacob's introduction to Pharaoh at the age of 130 years, the year 2238, marks the start of the 430-year sojourn (2108+130=2238). For the end of that sojourn, progress forward 430 years to the Exodus event, "even the selfsame day" in 2668 (2238+430=2668).

Exod. 7:7: *"And Moses was <u>fourscore years old</u>, and Aaron <u>fourscore and three years old,</u> when they spake unto Pharaoh."*

83.	Moses @ 80 spoke to Pharaoh; Egypt judged	2668	1332
	Aaron @ 83 spoke to Pharaoh		

Exod. 12:2–7:

This month shall be unto you the beginning of months: it shall be <u>the first month of the year</u> to you. Speak ye unto all the congregation of Israel, Saying, In the <u>tenth day of this month</u> they

shall take to them every man a lamb, according to the house of their fathers, a lamb for an house:
... And ye shall keep it up until <u>the fourteenth day of the same month</u>: and the whole assembly of
the congregation of Israel shall kill it in the evening. And they shall take of the blood, and strike
it on the two side posts and on the upper door post of the houses, wherein they shall eat it.

84. EXODUS 14th day, 1st month   2668   1332
   Later the same year, the law was given;
   End of 430-year sojourn period

Exod. 40:17: *"And it came to pass in the <u>first month in the second year, on the first day of the month,</u>*
that the tabernacle was reared up."

85. The Tabernacle was reared up 1st day, 1st   2669   1331
   month, 2nd year

Num. 9:1–3: *"And the LORD spake unto Moses in the wilderness of Sinai, in the <u>first month of the sec-</u>*
<u>ond year after they were come out of the land of Egypt</u>, saying, Let the children of Israel also keep the Passover
at his appointed season. In the <u>fourteenth day of this month</u>, at even, ye shall keep it in his appointed season:
according to all the rites of it, and according to all the ceremonies thereof, shall ye keep it."

86. Israel kept Passover 14th day, 1st month, 2nd   2669   1331
   year

Deut. 1:22–23: *"And ye came near unto me every one of you, and said, We will send men before us, and*
they shall search us out the land, and bring us word again by what way we must to up, and into what cities we
shall come. And the saying pleased me well: and I took twelve men of you, one of a tribe."
This account relates the incident as if the people instigated the spying operation, Moses being agreeable. The account in Num. 13:1–3 relates the operation as being of God only. Concerning
dates, we assume the spying operation to be within the second year after the Exodus. Also, we assume the forty-year judgment of Num. 14:33–34 to include the time interval from the Exodus event
until this same pronouncement: *"And your children shall wander in the wilderness <u>forty years</u>, and bear*
your whoredoms, until your carcasses be wasted in the wilderness. After the number of the days in which ye
searched the land, even forty days, each day for a year, shall ye bear your iniquities, even <u>forty years</u>, and ye
shall know my breach of promise."

87. Twelve spies search the land   2669   1331

Num. 33:38–39: *"And Aaron the priest went up into mount Hor at the commandment of the LORD, and died there, in the <u>fortieth year</u> after the children of Israel were come out of the land of Egypt, in the <u>first day of the fifth month</u>. And Aaron was <u>an hundred and twenty and three years</u> old when he died in mount Hor."*

The account of Aaron's death in the fortieth year and the considerable history after his death lead us to understand that this fortieth year mentioned was not the ending year of the wilderness journey, that is, as reported from Num. 33:40 onward; similarly, Num. 20:29 onward to the passage over Jordan. The constraining fact is that Moses died at the ending year of the wilderness journey and he was 120 years of age. According to scripture, Aaron was three years senior to Moses. Exod. 7:7: *"And Moses was <u>fourscore years</u> old, and Aaron <u>fourscore and three years</u> old, when they spake unto Pharaoh."* That being the case, Moses and Aaron died within the same year, and that was within a year of the passage over Jordan.

88.	Aaron died @ 123, 1st day, 5th month, 40th year	2708	1292

Deut. 1:1–3: *"These be the words which Moses spake unto all Israel on this side Jordan in the wilderness, in the plain over against the Red sea, between Paran, and To-phel, and Laban, and Ha-ze-roth, and Di-za-bah. (There are eleven days' journey from Horeb by way of mount Seir unto Kadesh-bar-ne-a.) And it came to pass in the <u>fortieth year, in the eleventh month, on the first day of the month,</u> that Moses spake unto the children of Israel, according unto all that the LORD had given him in commandment unto them."*

Deut. 34:5–7: *"So Moses the servant of the LORD died there in the land of Moab, according to the word of the LORD. And he buried him in a valley in the land of Moab, over against Beth-peor: but no man knoweth of his sepulcher unto this day. And Moses was <u>an hundred and twenty years</u> old when he died: his eye was not dim nor his natural force abated."*

89.	Moses died @ 120, 11th or 12th month, 40th year	2708	1292

While the month of Moses' death is not given, we know from the sequence that he died the eleventh or twelfth month of that year. That being the case, Moses outlived Aaron six or seven months. Moses had given the review of all that pertained to their sojourn of forty years in the wilderness; concluding that review in the eleventh month of that fortieth year. Furthermore, after Moses' death, the children of Israel passed over Jordan the tenth day of the first month, encamped in the land of promise, and the fourteenth day of that first month kept the Passover as observed exactly forty years earlier.

Josh. 4:19, 5:10: *"And the people came up out of Jordan on the <u>tenth day of the first month,</u> and encamped in Gilgal, on the east border of Jericho. ...And the children of Israel encamped in Gilgal, and kept the Passover on the <u>fourteenth day of the month</u> at even in the plains of Jericho."*

90.	Israel crossed Jordan the 10th day, first month, and kept Passover the 14th day, first month; Jericho fell and a curse was pronounced		2709	1291
91.	At rest—end of war—land divided		2714	1286
92.	*Boaz born of Rachab, Father; Salom @ 72 2715-2643=72, age of Salom at son's birth	estimate	2715	1285

Caleb was eighty-five years old when he petitioned for the Hebron land grant. Josh. 14:10–15: "And now, behold, the LORD hath kept me (Caleb) alive, as he said, these _forty and five years_, even since the LORD spake this word unto Moses, while the children of Israel wandered in the wilderness: and now, lo, I am this day _fourscore and five years_ old. ...Now therefore give me this mountain, whereof the LORD spake in that day... And Joshua blessed him, and gave unto Caleb the son of Je-phun-neh Hebron for an inheritance." ...And the land had rest from war."

That was the year 2714 (2629+85=2714). Jericho had fallen and the land had rest from war.

The term _"and the land had rest"_ is associated with a forty-year time frame; in this instance, 2714 to 2754.

Josh. 15:15–17: "And unto Caleb the son of Je-phun-neh he gave a part among the children of Judah, according to the commandment of the LORD to Joshua, even the city of Arba the father of Anak, which city is Hebron. ...And Caleb said, He that smiteth Kir-jath-se-pher, and taketh it, to him will I give Ach-sah his daughter to wife. And Othniel the son of Kenaz, the brother of Caleb, took it: and he gave him Ach-sah his daughter to wife."

Later, after the death of Joshua, as per Judges 1:12–15, the identical statement is repeated. There is no disparity, being that the accounting in Judges is either an update or it was the time the matter was concluded. What is evident is that Othniel enters the leadership picture earlier than thought. At least the initiation of the contract, with Othniel's inclusion, was in the timeframe of the _"rest"_ in the year 2714. Joshua lived twenty-five years beyond this marker. In this study, Othniel entered as the person of significance who kept the rest.

We do not know the year Joshua was born nor the year he died. It is a reasonable conjecture that Joshua and Caleb were in the same age bracket. Joshua was probably younger, but we do not know that. Caleb was forty years old in the first year after the Exodus.

Josh. 14:7: "Forty years old was I when Moses the servant of the LORD sent me from Kadesh-bar-ne-a to espy out the land..."

Equating Joshua's age to be the same as Caleb's, we thus estimate Joshua to be thirty-nine years old at the Exodus event 2668, and the year 2629 as his birth (2668-39=2629). Thus Joshua's death would have been approximately the year 2739 (2629+110=2739).

Josh. 24:29: *"And it came to pass after these things, that Joshua the son of Nun, the servant of the LORD, died, being* <u>*an hundred and ten years*</u> *old."*

93.	Joshua died @ 110	estimate	2739	1261

The children of Israel were free of bondages until the time of Joshua's death and possibly ten years beyond. Josh. 24:31: *"And Israel served the LORD all the days of Joshua, and all the days of the elders that overlived Joshua, and which had known all the works of the LORD, that he had done for Israel."*

The approximation of Joshua's death was thirty years after crossing Jordan into the promised land in 2739 (2709 to 2739=30). It is inferred that the elders that "overlived" Joshua were his generation of men. The time of Israel's good behavior ended in the approximation of forty years after entering the promised land, in 2749 (2709+40=2749). That would be ten years after Joshua's death (2739 to 2749=10). An obvious exception was the eight years' interruption by Cushan at a time of Israel's discouragement, about the time of Joshua's death. These dates are approximations and could reasonably vary five years.

It is a reasonable conjecture that Cushan of Mesopotamia rose up as Israel vacillated about the time of the of Joshua's death. The year 2739 marks the estimated beginning of eight years' oppression by Cushan, king of Mesopotamia. That oppression would have been within the ending years of the forty years of peacekeeping of Othniel. The eight years of oppression would be 2739 to 2747. The forty years of rest attributed to Othniel thus included the eight years' oppression, or interruption, by Cushan. That eight years is included within the last fifteen years of Othniel's forty years of rest and judgeship.

As determined earlier, Othniel entered leadership approximately the year 2714, but his deliverance of the nation from the oppression of Cushan was his mark of "judge." He was God's instrument of deliverance and he was the person of transition from the law-givers to judges; judges because their acts of courage and deliverance was a verdict, statement, and judgment as to the cause of Israel's dreadful plight. Othniel was peacekeeper and judge for forty years.

Going from the Joshua text to the Judges text sees us struggling with difficult determinations. Dates given in Judges are not always consecutive. Necessarily, special attention is given to the narrative. Scriptural references regarding the time durations of Judges and the years' intervals are related, with one exception, as given in scripture. The years of oppression are given as inclusive of the tenure of the judge-of-record when the Jews failed and were oppressed. Those dates are given within parentheses. The one exception being the eighteen-year servitude to Eglon, king of Moab.

Regarding this exception, it is noteworthy that Moab had a kinship with Israel. A thoughtful look at their history together reveals essentially a non-hostile attitude.

Judges 3:7–9, 11:

And the children of Israel did evil in the sight of the LORD, and forgat the LORD their God, and served Baalim and the groves. Therefore the anger of the LORD was hot against Israel, and he sold them into the hand of Chushan-rishathaim king of Mesopotamia: and the children of Israel served Chushan-rishathaim <u>eight years.</u> And when the children of Israel cried unto the LORD, the LORD raised up a deliverer to the children of Israel, who delivered them, even Othniel the son of Kenaz, Caleb's younger brother.... And the land had rest <u>forty years.</u> And Othniel the son of Kenaz died.

Othniel was peacekeeper, then judge from 2714 to 2754.

94.	40 years' rest under Othniel, younger brother of Caleb.		<u>2714</u>–2754	1286
95.	8 years' oppression by Cushan	estimate	(2739–2747)	1261

Judges 3:12, 14: *"And the children of Israel did evil again in the sight of the LORD: And the LORD strengthened Eglon the king of Moab against Israel, because they had done evil in the sight of the LORD... So the Children of Israel served Eglon the king of Moab <u>eighteen years</u>."*

96.	18 years' servitude to Eglon, king of Moab	<u>2754</u>–2772	1246

Judges 3:15, 30–31: *"But when the children of Israel cried unto the LORD, the LORD raised them up a deliverer, Ehud the son of Gera, a Benjamite, a man left-handed... So Moab was subdued that day under the hand of Israel. And the land had rest <u>fourscore years.</u> And after him was Shamgar the son of Anath, which slew of the Philistines six hundred men with an ox goad: and he also delivered Israel."*

The words *"the land had rest"* is expressed four times in Judges (3:11, 30; 5:31, 8:28). The forty-year figure is attached to all, excepting this verse, where it is ascribed, "fourscore years." The Greek text adds, "until he died." Nowhere in scripture is such an eighty-year tenure ascribed to one man. A forty-year tenure as judge is more acceptable, being the total "rest" was, in effect, eighty years up to that time, which would include the prior forty years of rest under Othniel. Duly noted, we will use the time of Ehud's judgeship as forty years, not eighty.

97.	40 years' rest under Ehud, a Benjamite.	<u>2772</u>–2812	1228

Judges 4:1–3: *"And the children of Israel again did evil in the sight of the LORD, when Ehud was dead. And the LORD sold them into the hand of Jabin king of Canaan, that reigned in Hazor; the captain of whose host was Sisera, which dwelt in Harosheth of the Gentiles. And the children of Israel cried unto the LORD: for he had nine hundred chariots of iron; and <u>twenty years</u> he mightily oppressed the children of Israel."*

98.	20 years' oppression by Jabin, king of Canaan.		(<u>2812</u>–2832)	1188

Judges 4:4, 5:31: *"And Deborah, a prophetess, the wife of Lapidoth, she judged Israel at the time.... So let all thine enemies perish, O LORD: but let them that love him be as the sun when he goeth forth in his might. And the land had rest <u>forty years</u>."*

99.	40 years' rest under Barak		<u>2812</u>–2852	1188

100.	*Obed born of Ruth; father Boaz @ 99	estimate	2814	1186
	2814–2715=99, age of Boaz at son's birth			

Judges 6:1: *"And the children of Israel did evil in the sight of the LORD: and the LORD delivered them into the hand of Midian <u>seven years</u>."*

101.	7 years delivered into the hand of the Midianites		(<u>2845</u>–2852)	1155

Judges 8:28: *"Thus was Midian subdued before the children of Israel, so that they lifted up their heads no more. And the country was in quietness <u>forty years</u> in the days of Gideon."*

102.	40 years' rest under Gideon		<u>2852</u>–2892	1148

Judges 8:33–35, 9:56:

And it came to pass, as soon as Gideon was dead, that the children of Israel turned again, and went a whoring after Baalim and made Baal-be-rith their god. And the children of Israel remembered not the LORD their God, who had delivered them out of the hands of all their enemies on every side: Neither shewed they kindness to the house of Jer-ub-ba-al, namely, Gideon, according to all the goodness which he had shewed unto Israel...And all the men of She-chem gathered together, and all the house of Millo, and went, and made A-bim-e-lech king.... When A-bim-e-lech had reigned <u>three years</u> over Israel. Then God sent an evil spirit between A-bim-e-lech and the men of She-chem... Thus God rendered the wickedness of A-bim-e-lech which he did unto his father, in slaying his seventy brethren.

103. 3 years' usurpation by Abimelech;   (2891–2894)   1109
call it year 2891

Judges 10:1–2: *"And after Abimelech there arose to defend Israel Tola the son of Puah, the son of Dodo, a man of Issachar; and he dwelt in Shamir in mount Ephraim. And he judged Israel twenty and three years, and died, and was buried in Shamir."*

104. 23 years under Tola of Issachar   2894–2917   1106

105. *Jessie born of Obed @ 90   estimate   2904   1096
2904–2814=90, age of Obed at son's birth

106. Eli born   2912   1088

Judges 10:3: *"And after him arose Jair, a Gileadite, and judged Israel twenty and two years."*

107. 22 years under Jair, a Gileadite.   2917–2939   1083

Judges 10:6–8:

And the children of Israel did evil again in the sight of the LORD, and served Baalim and Ashtaroth, and the gods of Syria, and the gods of Zidon, and the gods of Moab, and the gods of the children of Ammon, and the gods of the Philistines, and forsook the LORD, and served not him. And the anger of the LORD was hot against Israel, and he sold them into the hands of the Philistines, and into the hands of the children of Ammon. And that year they vexed and oppressed the children of Israel: eighteen years, all the children of Israel that were on the other side Jordan in the land of the Amorites, which is in Gilead.

108. 18 years' oppression by Ammonites   (2921–2939)   1079

Judges 12:7: *"And Jephthah judged Israel six years. Then died Jephthah the Gileadite, and was buried in one of the citied of Gilead."*

109. 6 years under Jephthah, the Gileadite   2939–2945   1061

Judges 12:8–9: *"And after him Ibzan of Bethlehem judged Israel. And he had thirty sons, and thirty daughters, whom he sent abroad, and took in thirty daughters from abroad for his sons. And he judged Israel seven years."*

110.   7 years under Ibzan of Bethlehem   <u>2945</u>–2952   1055

Judges 12:11: "And after him Elon, a Zebulonite, judged Israel; and he judged Israel <u>ten years</u>."

111.   10 years under Eglon, a Zebulonite   <u>2952</u>–2962   1048

Judges 12:13–14: "And after him Abdon the son of Hillel, a Pirathonite, judged Israel. And he had forty sons and thirty nephews, that rode on threescore and ten ass colts: and he judged Israel <u>eight years</u>."

112.   8 years under Abdon, a Pirathonite   <u>2962</u>–2970   1038

Judges 13:1–2, 24, 15:20: "And the children of Israel did evil again in the sight of the LORD; and the LORD delivered them into the hand of the Philistines <u>forty years</u>. And there was a certain man of Zorah, of the family of the Danites, whose name was Manoah; and his wife was barren, and bare not... And the woman bare a son, and called his name Samson: and the child grew, and the LORD blessed him... And <u>he judged Israel in the days of the Philistines twenty years</u>."

113.   40 years delivered into hands of Philistines;   <u>2970</u>–3010   1030
          Samson judged 20 years during the time of
          Philistine rule

Saul's choice as king was not God's perfect will but rather a result of the cries and demands of the people. Saul's time as king marks the beginning of the "Domain of the Kings," but it was marked with disobedience and sin. The beginning of Saul's reign in the year 2984 did not mark the end of the forty-year oppression by Israel's enemies, the Philistines and the Ammonites.

1 Sam. 4:15, 18: *"Now Eli was <u>ninety and eight years</u> old; and his eyes were dim, that he could not see. 18. And it came to pass, when he made mention of the ark of God, that he from off the seat backward by the side of the gate, and his neck brake, and he died: for he was an old man, and heavy. And he had judged Israel <u>forty years</u>."*

Calculating the beginning of Eli's forty-year judgeship: The ark was absent twenty years and ten months (twenty-one years), and that absence began at the same time Eli died. As mentioned in verse 18 above, it was the taking of the ark that marked Eli's death. The twenty years ten months' absence of the ark is determined thus: The ark was *"in the country of the Philistines <u>seven months</u>"* (1 Sam. 6:1). *"And it came to pass, while the ark abode in Kir-jath-je-a-rim, that the time was long; for it was <u>twenty years</u>: and all the house of Israel lamented after the LORD"* (1 Sam. 7:2). *"And the ark of the LORD continued in the house of Obed-edom the Gittite <u>three months</u>"* (2 Sam. 6:11). (7 months+20 years+3 months=20 years and 10 months; call it 21 years)

The ark was returned to Jerusalem the year King David moved his throne from Hebron to Jerusalem, the year 3031. Backdate twenty-one years from 3031 to give the year of the Ark's capture and Eli's death; also the year of beginning of the *"days"* of Samuel and the Philistine's decisive defeat, ending forty years of Philistine domination. That would be the year 3010 (3031-21=3010). Recounting: Philistine dominion of forty years, from 2970 to 3010.

Regarding Eli's birth and death: As determined, Eli died in the year 3010. Subtracting his lifespan of ninety-eight years from the year of his death, we arrive at 2912 as the year of Eli's birth (3010-98=2912). If Eli's forty-year judgeship ended when he died, then his judgeship began 2970 (2912+58=2970), when he was fifty-eight years of age (98-40=58). While it is conjecture, more likely, Eli's effectual judgeship began earlier and ended years before his death. That would mean that Samuel was the acting counsel during the last years of Eli's life. An overriding consideration is that Samuel was that transition person from judge to prophet. Samuel was God's instrument in orchestrating Saul's kingship in the year 2984. That would have been twenty-six years before Eli died (2984 to 3010=26). Samuel died in the timeframe of Saul's defeat and death, approximating the year 3024. Samuel's sole judgeship would have been from Eli's death in 3010, onward to the year of his and Saul's death in the year 3024; a span of fourteen years (3010 to 3024=14).

114.	40 years under Eli	<u>2970</u>–3010	1030
115.	Saul begins 40-year reign as king; Beginning of Kings' Dominions	2984	1016
116.	*David born of Jessie @ 90 2994-2904=90, age of Jessie at son's birth	2994	1006

Refreshing the point: Explicit dates of Samuel's judgeship are not given, and in the overview of the chronological chart of years, it seems to be a non-factor. However, treating the chronology more carefully, there is the need to know the time of beginning, *"All the days of Samuel."* The reason being that "beginning" marks the end of forty years of Philistine domination.

We do know from the text in 1 Samuel that Eli's death was coincidental with the taking of the ark. We know approximately twenty-one years expired before the ark was introduced back into the Jerusalem location. That event was in the year 3031, when David began to reign in Jerusalem. Backdating twenty-one years, we have the year of Eli's death, 3010 (3031-21=3010). The end of the forty years of Philistine rule will be thus dated as 3010. The beginning of the forty-year Philistine rule would be 2970 (3010-40=2970).

Regarding the end of that forty-year Philistine dominion: God wrought a great and decisive victory over the Philistines. According to the narrative beginning 1 Samuel 7, the victory and Samuel's "days," was about twenty-one years before the ark's return and within the year of Eli's death, the year 3010.

1 Sam. 7:12–13: *"Then Samuel took a stone, and set it between Mizpeh and Shen, and called the name of it Eben-ezer, saying, 'Hitherto hath the LORD helped us.' So the Philistines were subdued, and they came no more into the coast of Israel: and the hand of the LORD was against the Philistines all the days of Samuel."*

1 Sam. 4:18: *"And he (Eli) died: for he was an old man, and heavy. And he had judged Israel <u>forty years</u>."*

117.	Philistines take the ark of God, beginning 21 years' absence; Eli died @ 98; Decisive Philistine defeat, ending 40 years' domination.	3010	990

1 Sam. 7:2–3,11–13:

And it came to pass, while the ark abode in Kirjath-jearim, that the time was long; for it was <u>twenty years</u>: and all the house of Israel lamented after the LORD. And Samuel spake unto all the house of Israel, saying, If ye do return unto the LORD with all your hearts, then put away the strange gods and Ashtaroth from among you, and prepare your hearts unto the LORD, and serve him only: and he will deliver you out of the hand of the Philistines... And the men of Israel went out of Mizpeh, and pursued the Philistines, and smote them, until they came under Beth-car. Then Samuel took a stone, and set it between Mizpeh and Shen, and called the name of it Eben-ezer, saying, Hitherto hath the LORD helped us. So the Philistines were subdued, and they came no more into the coast of Israel: and the hand of the LORD was against the Philistines all the days of Samuel.

1 Sam. 7:15: *"And Samuel judged Israel all the days of his life."*

118.	Samuel died	estimate	3024	976
119.	Saul died in battle		3024	976

2 Sam. 5:4–5: *"David was <u>thirty years old</u> when he began to reign, and <u>he reigned forty years</u>. In Hebron he reigned over Judah <u>seven years and six months</u>: and in Jerusalem he reigned <u>thirty and three years</u> over all Israel and Judah."*

1 Kings 2:11: *"And the days that David reigned over Israel were <u>forty years</u>: <u>seven years</u> reigned he in Hebron, <u>and thirty and three years</u> reigned he in Jerusalem."*

120.	David @ 30 begins 40-year reign as king, reigning initially in Hebron 7½ years.	<u>3024</u>–3031	976
121.	David reigns in Jerusalem 33 years; The ark was returned after 21 years 3010+21=3031	<u>3031</u>–3064	969

We do not know the exact year of Solomon's birth. We do know from the narrative that Solomon was born approximately three years into David's reign in Jerusalem. That would be 3031+3=3034. Furthermore, we also know that Solomon's son, Rehoboam, was born forty-one years before Solomon's death. That is, Rehoboam was forty-one when he began to reign, which was the time of Solomon's death. It is reasonable that Solomon was a mature twenty-five year old when he bore his son Rehoboam. We estimate Solomon to have been born in 3034, when David was approximately forty-three years old.

122.	*Solomon born of David @ 40 3034-2994=40, age of David at son's birth	estimate	3034	966
123.	*Rehoboam born of Solomon @ 29 3063-3034=29, age of Solomon at son's birth	estimate	3063	937
124.	David died		3064	936

1 Kings 11:42: *"And the time that Solomon reigned in Jerusalem over all Israel was <u>forty years</u>."*

125.	Solomon begins 40-year reign as king	3064	936

1 Kings 6:1: *"AND it came to pass in the <u>four hundred and eightieth year</u> after the children of Israel were come out of the land of Egypt, in the <u>fourth year</u> of Solomon's reign over Israel, in the month Zif, which is the second month, that he began to build the house of the LORD."*

126.	Solomon's temple begun; End of 480-year period of 1 Kings 6:1	3068	932

1 Kings 8:6, 10–11: *"And the priests brought in the ark of the covenant of the LORD into his place, into the oracle of the house, to the most holy place, even under the wings of the cherubims.... And it came to pass, when the priests were come out of the holy place, that the cloud filled the house of the LORD. So that the priests could not stand to minister because of the cloud: for the glory of the LORD had filled the house of the LORD."*

1 Kings 9:1–7:

And it came to pass, when Solomon had finished the building of the house of the LORD, and king's house, and all Solomon's desire which he was pleased to do, That the LORD appeared to Solomon the second time, as he had appeared unto him at Gibeon.... And if thou wilt walk before me, as David thy father walked, in integrity of heart, and in uprightness, to do according to all that I have commanded thee, and wilt keep my statutes and my judgments: Then I will establish the throne of thy kingdom upon Israel for ever, as I promised to David thy father, saying, There shall not fail thee a man upon the throne of Israel. But if ye shall at all turn from following me, ye or your children, and will not keep my commandments and my statutes which I have set before you, but go and serve other gods, and worship them: Then will I cut off Israel out of the land which I have given them; and this house, which I have hallowed for my name, will I cast out of my sight; and Israel shall be a proverb and a byword among all people.

127.	Solomon's Temple completed; Later, the dedication		<u>3075</u>–3076	925
128.	The dedication, with statements of beginnings, glory, and judgment; Begin 390 years of Ezek. 4:5		3076	924
129.	*Abijam born of Rehoboam @ 20 3083-3063=20, age of Rehoboam at son's birth	estimated	3083	917
130.	Solomon died; Rehoboam reigns initially in his stead		3104	896

1 Kings 14:21: *"And Rehoboam the son of Solomon reigned in Judah. Rehoboam was <u>forty and one years old</u> when he began to reign, and he reigned <u>seventeen years</u> in Jerusalem..."*

131.	Rehoboam @ 41 begins 17-year reign		3104	896
132.	Nation divides: Judah to Rehoboam, Israel to Jeroboam		3104	896

1 Kings 14:20: *"And the days which Jeroboam reigned were <u>two and twenty years</u>."*

133.	Jeroboam begins 22-year reign over Israel		3104	896

1 Kings 12:28–30: *"Whereupon the king took counsel, and made two calves of gold, and said unto them, It is too much for you to go up to Jerusalem: behold thy gods, O Israel, which brought thee up out of the land of Egypt. And he set the one in Bethel, and the other put he in Dan. And this thing became a sin: for the people went to worship before the one, even unto Dan."*

134.	Jeroboam turns Israel to idol worship	3104	896

1 Kings 13:2: *"And he cried against the altar in the word of the LORD, and said, O altar, altar, thus saith the LORD; Behold, a child shall be born unto the house of David, Josiah by name; and upon thee shall he offer the priests of the high places that burn incense upon thee, and men's bones shall be burnt upon thee."*

135.	Prophecy to Jeroboam and Israel; Josiah mentioned		3104	896
136.	*Asa born of Abijam @ 25 3108-3083=25, age of Abijam at son's birth	estimate	3108	892

1 Kings 14:25–26: *"And it came to pass in the <u>fifth year</u> of king Rehoboam, that Shishak king of Egypt came up against Jerusalem: And he took away the treasures of the house of the LORD, and the treasures of the king's house; he even took away all: and he took away all the shields of gold which Solomon had made."*

137.	Shishak of Egypt spoiled/claimed parts of Judah	3109	891

1 Kings 14:31: *"And Rehoboam slept with his fathers, and was buried with his fathers in the city of David. And his mother's name was Naamah an Ammonitess. And Abijam his son reigned in his stead."*

138.	Rehoboam died	3121	879

1 Kings 15:1–2: *"Now in the <u>eighteenth year</u> of king Jeroboam the son of Nebat reigned Abijam over Judah. 2. <u>Three years</u> reigned he in Jerusalem."*
(3104+18=3122) (3122+3=3125; call it 3124) That is: Abijam reigned from 3122 to 3124.

139.	Abijam begins 3-year reign over Judah; 18th of Jeroboam	3122	878
140.	Abijam died	3124	876

1 Kings 15:9–10: *"And in the <u>twentieth year of Jeroboam</u> king of Israel reigned Asa over Judah. 10. And <u>forty and one years</u> reigned he in Jerusalem."*

(3104+20=3124) (3124+41=3165) That is: Asa reigned from 3124 to 3165.

141.	Asa begins 41-year reign over Judah; 20th of Jeroboam	3124	876
142.	Jeroboam died	3126	874

1 Kings 15:25, 28: *"And Nadab the son of Jeroboam began to reign over Israel in the <u>second year of Asa</u> king of Judah, and reigned over Israel <u>two years</u>. Even in the <u>third year of Asa</u> king of Judah did Baasha slay him, and reigned in his stead."*

(3124+2=3126; 3124+3=3127) That is: Nadab reigned from 3126 to 3127.

143.	Nadab begins 2-year reign over Israel	3126	874
144.	Nadab slain by Baasha	3127	873

1 Kings 15:33: *"In the <u>third year</u> of Asa king of Judah began Baasha the son of Ahijah to reign over all Israel in Tirzah, <u>twenty and four years</u>."*
(3124+3=3127) (3127+24=3151) That is: Baasha reigned from 3127 to 3151.

145.	Baasha begins 24-year reign over all Israel in Tirzah; 3rd of Asa	3127	873
146.	*Jehoshaphat born of Asa @ 23 3131-3108=23, age of Asa at son's birth	3131	869
147.	Asa calls great offering and makes covenant with God	3139	861
148.	Baasha died	3150	850

1 Kings 16:8, 10: *"In the <u>twenty and sixth year</u> of Asa king of Judah began Elah the son of Baasha to reign over Israel in Tirzah, <u>two years</u>. And Zimri went in and smote him, and killed him, in the <u>twenty and seventh year</u> of Asa king of Judah, and reigned in his stead."*

(3124+26=3150) (3150+2=3152) (3124+27=3151) That is: Elah reigned from 3150 to 3151.

149.	Elah begins 2-year reign over Israel in Tirzah; 26th of Asa	3150	850

150. Elah slain by Zimri   3151   849

1 Kings 16:15–18:

In the <u>twenty and seventh year</u> of Asa king of Judah did Zimri reign <u>seven days</u> in Tirzah. And the people were encamped against Gibbethon, which belonged to the Philistines. And the people that were encamped heard say, Zimri hath conspired, and hath also slain the king: wherefore all Israel made Omri, the captain of the host, king over Israel <u>that day</u> in the camp. And Omri went up from Gibbethon, and all Israel with him, and they besieged Tirzah. And it came to pass, when Zimri saw that the city was taken, that he went into the palace of the King's house, and burnt the king's house over him with fire, and died.

(3124+27=3151) (3151+7 days=3151) That is: Zimri reigned in Tirzah seven days (Zimri is part of the historical account, but no dates are given for his short tenure).

1 Kings 16:21–23: *"Then were the people of Israel divided into two parts: half of the people followed Tibni the son of Ginath, to make him King; and half followed Omri. But the people that followed Omri prevailed against the people that followed Tibni the son of Ginath: so Tibni died, and Omri reigned. In the <u>thirty and first year</u> of Asa king of Judah began Omri to reign over Israel, <u>twelve years</u>: <u>six years</u> reigned he in Tirzah."*

(Tibni is part of the historical account, but no dates are given for his short tenure.)

(3124+31=3155; call it 3156) (3156+6=3162) (3124+31+12=3167)

151. Omri begins 6 of 12 years' reign in Tirza   3151   849

152. Omri begins 6-year reign after Tirzah;   3156   844
      31st of Asa

153. *Jehoram born of Jehoshaphat @ 26   3157   843
      3157-3131=26, age of Jehoshaphat at son's birth

154. Omri died   3162   838

1 Kings 16:29: *"And in the <u>thirty and eighth year</u> of Asa king of Judah began Ahab the son of Omri to reign over Israel: and Ahab the son of Omri reigned over Israel in Samaria <u>twenty and two years</u>."*

(3124+38=3162) (3162+22=3184) That is: Ahab reigned 3162 to 3184.

155. Ahab begins 22-year reign over Israel;   3162   838
      38th of Asa

| 156. | Asa died | | 3165 | 835 |

1 Kings 22:41–42: *"And Jehoshaphat the son of Asa began to reign over Judah in the <u>fourth year of Ahab</u> king of Israel. Jehoshaphat was <u>thirty and five years old</u> when he began to reign; and he reigned <u>twenty and five years</u> in Jerusalem."*

(3162+4=3166) (3166+25=3191) That is: Jehoshaphat reigned from 3166 to 3191.

| 157. | Jehoshaphat @ 35 begins 25-year reign over Judah | | 3166 | 834 |

Jehoshaphat born 3131 (3166-35=3131)

1 Kings 16:33–34: *"And Ahab made a grove; and Ahab did more to provoke the Lord God of Israel to anger than all the kings of Israel that were before him. In his days did Hiel the Bethelite build Jericho: he laid the foundation thereof in Abiram his firstborn, and set up the gates thereof in his youngest son Segub, according to the word of the Lord, which he spake by Joshua the son of Nun."*

"In his days" refers to the reign of Ahab, which would have been 3162–3183. Actually a span of twenty-two years explicitly, as per the text. Taking a midpoint of that span, we give an approximation for the "building project" of Jericho to be 3173. The prophecy by Joshua was spoken in 2709 (Josh. 6:26). That would be 464 years earlier.

| 158. | Jericho rebuilt | approximation | 3173 | 827 |

| 159. | *Ahaziah born of Jehoram @ 17 | | 3174 | 826 |

3174–3157=17, age of Jehoram at son's birth

| 160. | Ahab died after being smitten in battle | | 3183 | 817 |

1 Kings 22:40, 51: *"So Ahab slept with his fathers; and Ahaziah his son reigned in his stead. ... Ahaziah the son of Ahab began to reign over Israel in Samaria the <u>seventeenth year</u> of Jehoshaphat king of Judah, and reigned <u>two years</u> over Israel."*

(3166+17=3183) (3183+2=3185)

| 161. | Ahaziah begins 2-year reign over Israel; 17th of Jehoshaphat | | 3183 | 817 |

2 Kings 1:1–2, 4, 17: *"Then Moab rebelled against Israel after the death of Ahab. And Ahaziah fell down through a lattice in his upper chamber that was in Samaria, and was sick... Now therefore thus saith the LORD, Thou shalt not come down from that bed on which thou art gone up, but shalt surely die. And Elijah departed...*

So he died according to the word of the Lord which Elijah had spoken. And Jehoram reigned in his stead in the second year of Jehoram the son of Jehoshaphat king of Judah; because he had no son."

This Jehoram was a son of Ahab and brother (half-brother) to Ahaziah.

162.	Jehoram (Joram) begins 12-year reign over Israel	3184	816

163.	Ahaziah died after injury/disease	3185	815

It is not stated explicitly, but Ahaziah's injury allowed that his brother, Jehoram, co-reigned with him for one year and that one year is attributed to Jehoram's 12-year reign as mentioned.

2 Kings 3:1: *"Now Jehoram the son of Ahab began to reign over Israel in Samaria the eighteenth year of Jehoshaphat king of Judah, and reigned twelve years."*

(3166+18=3184) (3184+12=3196)

2 Kings 8:16–17: *"And in the fifth year of Joram the son of Ahab king of Israel, Jehoshaphat being then king of Judah, Jehoram the son of Jehoshaphat king of Judah began to reign. Thirty and two years old was he when he began to reign; and he reigned eight years in Jerusalem."* The statement, *"Jehoshaphat being then king of Judah,"* indicates a co-reign of Jehoram with his father Jehoshaphat.

(3184+5=3189) (3189+8=3197)

164.	Jehoram @ 32 begins 8-year reign over Judah Jehoram born in 3157 (3189-32=3157)	3189	811

165.	Jehoshaphat of Judah died	3191	809

166.	Jehoram (Joram) of Judah died, smitten of disease	3196	804

2 Kings 8:25–26: *"In the twelfth year of Joram the son of Ahab king of Israel did Ahaziah the son of Jehoram king of Judah begin to reign. Two and twenty years old was Ahaziah when he began to reign; and he reigned one year in Jerusalem."*

(3184+12=3196) (3196+1=3197)

167.	Ahaziah @ 22, reigned 1 year over Judah; 12th of Joram Ahaziah born in 3174 (3196-22=3174)	3196	804

168. *Joash, son of Ahaziah born @ 23   3197   803
     3197-3174=23, age of Ahaziah at son's birth

169. Jehoram (Joram) of Israel died, smitten by Jehu   3197   803

170. Ahaziah of Judah died, smitten by Jehu   3197   803

 2 Kings 10:35–36: *"And Jehu slept with his fathers: and they buried him in Samaria. And Jehoahaz his son reigned in his stead. And the time that Jehu reigned over Israel in Samaria was twenty and eight years."*
     (3197+28=3225)

171. Jehu begins 28-year reign over Israel   3197   803

 2 Kings 11:1–4:

And when Athaliah the mother of Ahaziah saw that her son was dead, she arose and destroyed all the seed royal. But Jehosheba, the daughter of king Joram, sister of Ahaziah, took Joash the son of Ahaziah, and stole him from among the king's sons which were slain; and they hid him, even him and his nurse, in the bedchamber from Athaliah, so that he was not slain. And he was with her hid in the house of the LORD six years. And Athaliah did reign over the land. And the seventh year Jehoiada sent and fetched the rulers... and shewed them the king's son.

 (3197+6=3203) (3198+7=3204)

172. Athaliah begins 6-year rule over Judah   3198   802

173. Athaliah died, slain by the sword   3204   796

 2 Kings 11:21; 12:1, 20–21: *"Seven years old was Jehoash when he began to reign. In the seventh year of Jehu Jehoash began to reign; and forty years reigned he in Jerusalem... And his servants arose, and made a conspiracy, and slew Joash...and they buried him with his fathers in the city of David: and Amaziah his son reigned in his stead."*
     (Jehoash=Joash. See 11:2. Son of Ahaziah.)
     (3197+7=3204) (3204+40=3244) That is: Joash reigned from 3204 to 3244.

174. Joash @ 7 begins 40-year reign over Judah   3204   796
     Joash born 3197 (3204-7=3197)

175.   *Amaziah, son of Joash, born @ 21   3218   782

3218-3197=21, age of Joash at son's birth

2 Kings 13:1, 9–10: *"In the three and twentieth year of Joash the son of Ahaziah King of Judah Jehoahaz the son of Jehu began to reign over Israel in Samaria, and reigned seventeen years... And Jehoahaz slept with his fathers; and they buried him in Samaria: and Joash his son reigned in his stead. In the thirty and seventh year of Joash king of Judah began Jehoash the son of Jehoahaz to reign over Israel in Samaria, and reigned sixteen years."*

Jehoahaz reigned seventeen years in Samaria. That begins in the 23rd year of Joash of Judah (2 Kings 13:1). Jehoahaz's son Jehoash (Joash) begins to reign in the 37th year of Joash of Judah (2 Kings 13:10). That is a difference of fourteen years and not the stated seventeen years, a difference of three years. It is noteworthy that in the record of the Kings, chapter 12, Jehoash's forty-year reign is first stated, and verse 6 states, *"In the three and twentieth year of king Jehoash* (Joash) *the priests had not repaired the breaches of the house."* That is a stated date of record and the chapter ends with the detail of Joash being smitten and replaced without a date. It is not unreasonable that the stated date of verse 6 was transferred to the opening statement of chapter 13 and for the sake of continuity. If we correct the twenty-three years of 2 Kings 13:1 to twenty years, the math proves correct. The correction may be an assumption; fortuitously, if so be, the correction is minor.

(3204+20=3224) (3224+17=3241) That is: The reign of Jehoahaz was 3224 to 3241.

(3204+37=3241) (3241+16=3257) That is: The reign of Jehoash was 3241 to 3257.

176.   Jehoahaz begins 17-year reign over Israel;   3224   776
       23rd year of Joash

177.   Jehu died   3225   775

178.   Jehoahaz of Israel died   3241   759

179.   Jehoash begins 16-year reign over Israel;   3241   759
       37th of Joash

180.   Joash of Judah died   3243   757

2 Kings 14:1–2: *"In the second year of Joash son of Jehoahaz king of Israel reigned Amaziah the son of Joash king of Judah. He was twenty and five years old when he began to reign, and reigned twenty and nine years in Jerusalem."* (See 2 Chron. 25:1.)

(3241+2=3243) (3243+29=3272) That is: the reign of Amaziah was 3243 to 3272.

181.	Amaziah @ 25 begins 29-year reign over Judah	3243	757
	Amaziah born 3218 (3243-25=3218)		
182.	*Uzziah (Azariah), son of Amaziah, born @ 36	3254	746
	3254-3218=36, age of Amaziah at son's birth		

2 Kings 14:8, 12–14:

Then Amaziah (of Judah) sent messengers to Jehoash (Joash of Israel), the son of Jehoahaz son of Jehu, king of Israel, saying, Come, let us look one another in the face... And Judah was put to the worse before Israel; and they fled every man to their tents. And Jehoash king of Israel took Amaziah king of Judah, the son of Ahaziah, at Bethshemesh, and came to Jerusalem, and brake down the wall of Jerusalem from the gate of Ephraim unto the corner gate, four hundred cubits. And he took all the gold and silver, and all the vessels that were found in the house of the LORD, and in the treasures of the king's house, and hostages, and returned to Samaria.

This passage in 2 Kings 14:8, 12–14 relates a tragic episode for Amaziah and the people of Judah. And, the debacle was at Amaziah's instigation. It resulted in the casting down of Amaziah to co-regent with his sixteen-year-old son, Azariah (Uzziah). To wit: 2 Kings 14:21, *"And all the people of Judah took Azariah (Uzziah), which was sixteen years old, and made him king instead of his father Amaziah."*

Second Kings 14:18–20 and 2 Chron. 25:27–28 gives the ending statement and detail of Amaziah's death. However, Amaziah was the continuing subject of the narrative so that this insertion does not take away from the narrative of Azariah being installed as co-regent with his father. Second Kings 14:14 connects directly to verse 21; and 2 Chron. 25:24 connects directly to 26:1.

From this treatment of the narrative, we determine that *"the people of Judah took Azariah (Uzziah), which was sixteen years old, and made him king instead of his father Amaziah"* in the years after the death of Jehoash. That would calculate to be the year 3261. So that Azariah was co-regent with his father for twelve years, 3261 to 3273, and then reigned solely forty years, 3273 to 3313. The two periods totaled 52 years.

What might be confusing to some is the fact that Amaziah of Judah reigned twenty-nine years and two periods of fifteen years come forth from that twenty-nine years' time frame. First, Amaziah outlived his opponent Joash of Israel by fifteen years. Also, it was in the 15th year of Amaziah that Jeroboam began to reign in Samaria at the death of his father Joash. Another twelve years is derived from the context as the time Azariah (Uzziah) was co-regent with his father Amaziah (3261 to 3273=12). At sixteen years of age, Azariah became co-regent for twelve years with his father Amaziah. That is twelve years before his father Amaziah's death in 3273.

(3261+12=3273) (3261+52=3313) That is: Azariah (Uzziah) died in 3313.

2 Kings 15:1–2: *"In the <u>twenty and seventh year</u> of Jeroboam king of Israel began Azariah (Uzziah) son of Amaziah king of Judah to reign. <u>Sixteen years old</u> was he when he began to reign, and he reigned <u>two and fifty rears</u> in Jerusalem."*

Reviewing the premise: Thoughtful consideration of the above text leads us to understand that the people installed Azariah twelve years before Amaziah actually died. So Azariah would have become co-regent with his father Amaziah in the 3rd year of Jeroboam of Israel (3258 to 3261=3), then reigning solely in the 15th year of Jeroboam (3258 to 3273=15). It is possible that the twelve years of Azariah's co-regency would have been mistakenly added to the fifteen-year figure. While the total would give the *"twenty and seventh year"* of 2 Kings 15:1, it would have been an incorrect deduction. Also, it is possible this twenty-seven-year figure was recorded as months and treated as years; confessedly, an unlikely conjecture. However, it renders a fitting approximation of three years—an unlikely conjecture.

2 Kings 14:15–17: *"Now the rest of the acts of Jehoash which he did, and his might, and how he fought with Amaziah king of Judah, are they not written in the book of the chronicles of the kings of Israel? And Jehoash slept with his fathers, and was buried in Samaria with the kings of Israel; and Jeroboam his son reigned in his stead. And Amaziah the son of Joash king of Judah lived after the death of Jehoash son of Jehoahaz king of Israel <u>fifteen years</u>."*

Amaziah outlived Jehoash of Israel fifteen years. That is, Jehoash of Israel died in 3258 and Amaziah died in 3273 (3258+15=3273).

183.	Jehoash of Israel died	3258	742

2 Kings 14:23: *"In the <u>fifteenth year</u> of Amaziah the son of Joash king of Judah Jeroboam the son of Joash king of Israel began to reign in Samaria, and reigned <u>forty and one years</u>."*

(3243+15=3258) (3258+41=3299) That is: The reign of Jeroboam was 3258 to 3299.

184.	Jeroboam begins 41-year reign over Israel; 15th of Amaziah	3258	742
185.	Azariah @ 16 reigns 12 years co-regent over Judah	3261	739
186.	Amaziah died 15 years after Jehoash of Israel	3273	727
187.	Azariah's reign continued 40 years as sole king of Judah	3273	727

188.   *Jotham, son of Azariah (Uzziah) born @ 36   3290   710
        3290-3254=36, age of Uzziah at son's birth

189.   Jeroboam (Israel) died   3299   701

        2 Kings 15:5: *"And the LORD smote the king, (Azariah) so that he was a leper unto the day of death, and dwelt in a several house. And Jotham the king's son was over the house, judging the people of the land."*

        2 Kings 15:8: *"In the <u>thirty and eighth year</u> of Azariah king of Judah did Zachariah the son of Jeroboam reign over Israel in Samaria <u>six months</u>."*

        (3261+38=3299) That is: Zachariah reigned for six months in the year's change 3299 to 3300.

190.   Zachariah reigns 6 months over Israel;   3299   701
        38th of Azariah

        2 Kings 15:10: *"And Shallum the son of Jabesh conspired against him, and smote him before the people, and slew him, and reigned in his stead."*

191.   Zachariah died, slain by Shallum   3300   700

        2 Kings 15:13: *"Shallum the son of Jabesh began to reign in the <u>nine and thirtieth year</u> of Uzziah King of Judah; and he reigned <u>a full month</u> in Samaria."*

        (3261+39=3300) That is: Shallum reigned within the year 3300.

192.   Shallum begins 1-month reign over Israel   3300   700

        2 Kings 15:14: *"For Menahem the son of Gadi went up from Tirzah, and came to Samaria, and smote Shallum the son of Jabesh in Samaria, and slew him, and reigned in his stead."*

193.   Shallum died, slain by Menahem   3300   700

        2 Kings 15:17: *"In the <u>nine and thirtieth year</u> of Azariah king of Judah began Menahem the son of Gadi to reign over Israel, and reigned <u>ten years</u> in Samaria."*

        (3261+39=3300) (3300+10=3310) That is: Menahem reigned from 3300 to 3310.

194.   Menahem begins 10-year reign over Israel;   3300   700
        39th of Azariah

195.   *Ahaz, son of Jotham, born @ 20   3310   690
        3310-3290=20, age of Jotham at son's birth

2 Kings 15:22: *"And Menahem slept with his fathers; and Pekahiah his son reigned in his stead."*

| 196. | Menahem died | 3310 | 690 |

2 Kings 15:23: *"In the fiftieth year of Azariah king of Judah Pekahiah the son of Menahem began to reign over Israel in Samaria, and reigned two years."*
(3261+50=3311) (3311+2=3313) That is: Pekahiah reigned from 3311 to 3313.

| 197. | Pekahiah begins 2-year reign over Israel; 50th of Uzziah | 3311 | 689 |

Isaiah 6:1: *"In the year that king Uzziah died I saw also the LORD sitting upon a throne, high and lifted up, and his train filled the temple."*

| 198. | Isaiah's vision | 3313 | 687 |

Amos 1:1; Zech.14:5: The time of Uzziah would be, in the bigger time span, from 3273 to 3313. Isaiah's vision was in the year Uzziah died, being 3313, and that particular time and event seems closely associated. It is arbitrary, but we will call it 3313.

| 199. | Great earthquake: | 3313 | 687 |
| 200. | Uzziah (Azariah) died | 3313 | 687 |

2 Kings 15:25: *"But Pekah the son of Remaliah, a captain of his, conspired against him, and smote him in Samaria, in the palace of the king's house, with Argob and Arieh, and with him fifty men of the Gileadites: and he killed him, and reigned in his room."*

| 201. | Pekahiah died, slain by Pekah | 3313 | 687 |

2 Kings 15:27: *"In the two and fiftieth year of Azariah king of Judah Pekah the son of Remaliah began to reign over Israel in Samaria, and reigned twenty years."*
(3261+52=3313) (3313+20=3333) That is: Pekah reigned from 3313 to 3333.

| 202. | Pekah begins 20-year reign over Israel | 3313 | 687 |

2 Kings 15:32–33: *"In the second year of Pekah the son of Remaliah king of Israel began Jotham the son of Uzziah king of Judah to reign. Five and twenty years old was he when he began to reign, and he reigned sixteen years in Jerusalem."*
(3313+2=3315) (3315+16=3331) That is: Jotham reigned from 3315 to 3331.

203.	Jotham @ 25 begins 16-year reign over Judah; 2nd of Pekah	3315	685
	Jotham born in 3290 (3315-25=3290)		
204.	*Hezekiah, son of Ahaz, born @ 11	3321	679
	3321-3310=11, age at son's birth		
205.	Jotham died	3330	670

2 Kings 16:1–2: *"In the <u>seventeenth year</u> of Pekah the son of Remaliah Ahaz the son of Jotham king of Judah began to reign. <u>Twenty years</u> old was Ahaz when he began to reign, and reigned <u>sixteen years</u> in Jerusalem..."*

(3313+17=3330) (3330+16=3346) That is: Ahaz reigned from 3330 to 3346.

206.	Ahaz @ 20 begins 16-year reign over Judah	3330	670
	Ahaz born in 3310 (3330-20=3310)		

2 Kings 15:30: *"And Hoshea the son of Elah made a conspiracy against Pekah the son of Remaliah, and smote him and slew him, and reigned in his stead, in the <u>twentieth year</u> of Jotham the son of Uzziah."* (3315+20=3335)

The above date of 3335 is two years later than the determined date of 3333. The twenty-year figure is suspect being that Jotham only reigned for sixteen years. Thus, we use 2 Kings 17:1 as the preferred scriptural basis for the 3333 date.

207.	Pekah died, slain by Hoshea	3333	667

BEGIN SIXTH ERA	3333	3333	667

2 Kings 17:1: *"In the <u>twelfth year</u> of Ahaz king of Judah began Hoshea the son of Elah to reign in Samaria over Israel <u>nine years</u>."*

(3330+12=3342) (3342+9=3351) That is: Hoshea reigned from 3342 to 3351.

208.	Hoshea begins 9-year reign over Israel	3342	658

2 Kings 16:20: *"And Ahaz slept with his fathers, and was buried with his fathers in the city of David: and Hezekiah his son reigned in his stead."*

209.	Ahaz died	3346	654

2 Kings 18:1–2: *"Now it came to pass in the third year of Hoshea son of Elah king of Israel, that Hezekiah the son of Ahaz king of Judah began to reign. Twenty and five years old was he when he began to reign; and he reigned twenty and nine years in Jerusalem."*

(3343+3=3346) (3346+29=3375) That is: Hezekiah reigned from 3346 to 3375.

210.	Hezekiah @ 25 begins 29-year reign over Judah; 3rd of Hoshea	3346	654

Hezekiah born in 3321 (3346−25=3321)

2 Kings 17:5–6: *"Then the king of Assyria came up throughout all the land, and went up to Samaria, and besieged it three years. In the ninth year of Hoshea the king of Assyria took Samaria, and carried Israel away into Assyria, and placed them in Halah and in Habor by the river of Gozan, and in the cities of the Medes."*

(3342+9=3351) (3351−3=3348) That is: Samaria was besieged from 3348 to 3351.

This time frame is given as per the reign of Hoshea, king over Israel. Second Kings 18:9–10 gives the same time frame based on both Hoshea, king of Israel, and Hezekiah, king of Judah. The dates are comparable and well within the acceptable range. Since the latter scripture is more comprehensive, we will use those dates.

To wit: 2 Kings 18:9–10 says, *"And it came to pass in the fourth year of king Hezekiah, which was the seventh year of Hoshea son of Elah king of Israel, that Shalmaneser king of Assyria came up against Samaria, and besieged it. And at the end of three years they took it: even in the sixth year of Hezekiah, that is the ninth year of Hoshea king of Israel, Samaria was taken."*

(3346+4=3350) (3342+7=3349) (3346+6=3352) (3342+9=3351)

That is: Samaria was besieged in 3349 and fell in 3352.

211.	Shalmaneser of Assyria besieges Samaria (Israel)	3349	651
212.	Samaria taken; end of northern kingdom (Israel); That is, being the 6th year of Hezekiah	3352	648
213.	Hezekiah healed and given 15 additional years	3360	640

2 Kings 18:13: *"Now in the fourteenth year of king Hezekiah did Sennacherib king of Assyria come up against all the fenced cities of Judah, and took them."*

(3346+14=3360)

214.	Judah besieged	3360	640

215.   *Manasseh, son of Hezekiah, born @ 42   3363   637
       3363-3321=42, age of Hezekiah at son's birth

   2 Kings 20:21: *"And Hezekiah slept with his fathers: and Manasseh his son reigned in his stead."*

216.   Hezekiah died   3375   625

   2 Kings 21:1: *"Manasseh was <u>twelve years</u> old when he began to reign, and reigned <u>fifty and five years</u> in Jerusalem."*
   (3375+55=3430) That is: Manasseh, son of Hezekiah, reigned from 3375 to 3430.

217.   Manasseh @ 12 begins 55-year reign   3375   625
       Manasseh born in 3363 (3375-12=3363)

218.   *Amon, son of Manasseh, born @ 45   3408   592
       3408-3363=45, age of Manasseh at son's birth

219.   *Josiah, son of Amon, born @ 16   3424   576
       3424-3408=16, age of Amon at son's birth

   2 Kings 21:18: *"And Manasseh slept with his fathers, and was buried in the garden of his own house, in the garden of Uzza: and Amon his son reigned in his stead."*

220.   Manasseh died   3430   570

   2 Kings 21:19: *"Amon was <u>twenty and two years</u> old when he began to reign, and he reigned <u>two years</u> in Jerusalem."*
   (3430+2=3432) That is: Amon reigned from 3430 to 3432.

221.   Amon @ 22 begins 2-year reign   3430   570
       Amon born in 3408 (3430-22=3408)

   2 Kings 21:23: *"And he (Amon) was buried in his sepulcher in the garden of Uzza: and Josiah his son reigned in his stead."*

222.   Amon died, slain by his servants   3432   568

   2 Kings 22:1: *"Josiah was <u>eight years</u> old when he began to reign, and he reigned <u>thirty and one years</u> in Jerusalem."*
   (3432+31=3463) That is: Josiah reigned from 3432 to 3463.

223.	Josiah @ 8 begins 31-year reign	3432	568
	Josiah born in 3424 (3432-8=3424)		
224.	*Jehoiakim, son of Josiah, born @ 14	3438	562
	3438-3424=14, age of Josiah at son's birth		
225.	Jehoahaz, son of Josiah, born @ 16	3440	560
	3440-3424=16, age of Josiah at son's birth		

Fourteen and then sixteen years of age is young for Josiah to sire children. Considering their situation and Josiah already being king for four years, marriage at age thirteen is feasible.

2 Chron. 34:3: *"For in the eight year of his reign, while he was yet young, he began to seek after the God of David his father: and in the twelfth year he began to purge Judah and Jerusalem from the high places, and the groves, and the carved images, and the molten images."*

(3432+8=3440) (3432+12=3444)

226.	Josiah @ 16 begins to seek God	3440	560
227.	Josiah @ 20 in his 13th year begins the purge;	3444	556
	Within a year, he fulfills 1 Kings 13:2		

At this time, the prophecy of 1 Kings 13:1–2 begins to be fulfilled: *"And behold, there came a man of God out of Judah by the word of the LORD unto Bethel: and Jeroboam stood by the altar to burn incense. And he cried against the altar in the word of the Lord, and said, O altar, altar, thus saith the LORD; Behold, a child shall be born unto the house of David, Josiah by name; and upon thee shall he offer the priests of the high places that burn incense upon thee, and men's bones shall be burnt upon thee."*

The fulfillment, to wit: 2 Kings 23:16: *"And as Josiah turned himself, he spied the sepulchers that were there in the mount, and sent, and took the bones out of the sepulchers, and burned them upon the altar, and polluted it, according to the word of the LORD which the man of God proclaimed, who proclaimed these words."*

Jer. 25:1, 3, 11:

The word that came to Jeremiah concerning all the people of Judah in the <u>fourth year</u> of Jehoiakim the son of Josiah king of Judah, that was the <u>first year of Nebuchadnezzar king of Babylon</u>.... From the <u>thirteenth year of Josiah the son of Amon king of Judah, even unto this day, that is the three and twentieth year</u>, the word of the LORD hath come unto me, and I have spoken unto you, rising early and speaking; but ye have not hearkened.... And this whole land shall be a desolation, and an astonishment; and these nations shall serve the king of Babylon <u>seventy years</u>.

For the reader's convenience, this scripture is repeated at item 238.

(3432+13=3445) (3445+23=3468) (Verse 1 refers to end point: 3463+4=3467)

228.	The time of Jeremiah warning *"all the people of Judah"*; Fulfilled prophecies: 2 Kings 13:2, 23:26–27; Begin 40 years of Ezek. 4:6	3445	555

2 Kings 22:3: *"And it came to pass in the <u>eighteenth year</u> of King Josiah, that the king sent Shaphan the son of Azaliah, the son of Meshullam, the scribe , to the house of the LORD..."*

The narrative begins with attention being centered on the *"house of the LORD."* The story progresses to reveal that Hilkiah the priest became involved, found the book of the law, and passed it to Shaphan the scribe who read it to the king. Verse 13 states the king's conviction: *"Go ye, enquire of the LORD for me, and for the people, and for all Judah, concerning the words of this book that is found: for great is the wrath of the LORD that is kindled against us, because our fathers have not hearkened unto the words of this book, to do according unto all that which is written concerning us."*

(3432+18=3450)

229.	Josiah initiates final, urgent actions, hoping for a remedy	3450	550

2 Kings 23:23: *"But in the <u>eighteenth year</u> of King Josiah, wherein this Passover was holden to the LORD in Jerusalem."*

(3432+18=3450)

230.	Purge completed; the great Passover was the 18th year	3450	550

2 Kings 23:26–27: *"Notwithstanding the LORD turned not from the fierceness of his great wrath, wherewith his anger was kindled against Judah, because of all the provocations that Manasseh had provoked him withal. And the LORD said, I will remove Judah also out of my sight, as I have removed Israel, and will cast off this city Jerusalem which I have chosen, and the house of which I said, My name shall be there."*

This is the Lord's verdict on Judah. God's judgment is thus set forth. The date starting this verdict is 3450. Josiah's determination has the 3444 date, which was the start of the purge and year 3445 as fulfilling the details of the prophecy of 1 Kings 13:1–2. Ezekiel demonstrates this determination in Ezek. 4:6: *"Lie again on thy right side, and thou shalt bear the iniquity of the house of Judah forty days: I have appointed thee each day for a year."* This date rightfully begins the forty years of Ezek. 4:6. This fact further reveals that God determined Judah's judgment even from the onset of Josiah's efforts five years earlier when he burned the bones of the false priest on the altar. Going forward forty years brings us to the year 3485 (3445+40=3485), the destruction of Jerusalem and the Temple.

Josiah was a good king and his death, thirteen years later, seemed untimely. Jeremiah wept for Josiah and Judah. Perhaps Josiah was more righteous than Judah's estate allowed, considering the pending righteous judgment of God.

231. Zedekiah, son of Josiah, uncle to Jehoiachin,   3453   547
      born @ 29
      3453-3424=29, age of Josiah at son's birth

232. *Jehoiachin, son of Jehoiakim, born @ 18   3456   544
      3456-3438=18, age of Jehoiakim at son's birth
      *Jeconiah, son of Jehoiakim born @ 18   estimated   3456   544
      3456-3438=18, age of Jehoiakim at son's birth

Scripture makes no place for separate persons Jehoiachin and Jeconiah. However, without proof-positive that they are one and the same, it is treated as "undecided." The matter is expressed thus: Jehoiachin is the end of the kingly line and Jeconiah is the bloodline descendant of the same generation. Zedekiah is dealt out of the kingly line for two reasons. First, he entered by appointment when the continuity of the nation was ceased and under Babylonian rule. Furthermore, he was reproached and brutalized by that same Babylonian rule. Secondly, scripture shows Jehoiachin to be the last out (2 Kings 25:27–30).

2 Chron. 3:15–19: "And the sons of <u>Josiah</u> were, the firstborn Johanan, the second <u>Jehoiakim</u>, the third Zedekiah, the fourth Shallum. And the sons of Jehoiakim: <u>Jeconiah (Jechonias)</u> his son, Zedekiah his son. And the sons of Jeconiah; <u>Assir</u> (captive), <u>Salathiel</u> his son, Malchiram also, and Pedaiah, and Shenazar, Jecamiah, Hoshama, and Nedabiah. And the sons of Pedaiah were, <u>Zerubbabel</u>, and Shimei: and the sons of Zerubbabel; Meshullam, and Hananiah, and Shelomith their sister."

Regarding the preceding chronology: first, Jehoiakim and Pedaiah are listed but omitted in Matthew's chronology. Zerubbabel is listed as the son of Pedaiah when both Matt. 1:12 and Luke 3:27 give Salathiel as begetting Zerubbabel. We will concede the matter of kingly lineage to Matthew and Luke, but the above blood lineage includes Pedaiah. That is: Salathiel, then Pedaiah, and then Zerubbabel. Third, a question may arise as to whether Zedekiah, the son of Josiah, or Zedekiah, the son of Jeconiah, was a replacement to Jehoiachin, as per 2 Kings 24:17. Scripture decidedly favors Zedekiah being the uncle to Jehoiachin and not his son. Again, Jehoiachin, who was king for three months in Jerusalem and is given last mention in 2 Kings 25:27–30.

The blood line goes from Josiah, then <u>Jehoiakim</u>, then <u>Jeconiah</u> (Jechonias), the same as or brother to Jehoiachin, then <u>Salathiel</u> of the captivity, then <u>Pedaiah</u>, and then <u>Zerubbabel</u>. According to 1 Chron. 3:16, Jeconiah is listed as the son of Jehoiakim and if Jeconiah was brother to Jehoiachin, then Jeconiah was in the blood line but not in the kingly line. He is given an estimated birth date of 3456. Matt. 1:11 leaves Jehoiakim unmentioned but he is in the blood line lineage. We are estimating dates of birth so that the estimated date of birth for Jeconiah will be 3456, same as Jehoiachin whose birth date is given. The underlying question remains as to if they are one and the same person.

This chronology chart gives both Jeconiah and Jehoiachin the notation as being in the blood line lineage of Christ. On that point, if brothers, there is no difference and substitution is valid.

2 Kings 23:29: *"In his days Pharaoh-nechoh king of Egypt went up against the king of Assyria to the river Euphrates: and king Josiah went against him; and he slew him at Megiddo, when he had seen him."*

| 233. | Josiah died, slain by Pharaoh Nechoh | 3463 | 537 |

2 Kings 23:30–31: *"And the people of the land took Jehoahaz the son of Josiah, and anointed him, and made him king in his father's stead. Jehoahaz was twenty and three years old when he began to reign; and he reigned three months in Jerusalem."*

(3463+3 months=3463) That is: Jehoahaz reigned in the year 3463.

| 234. | Jehoahaz @ 23 begins 3-month reign | 3463 | 537 |
| | Jehoahaz born in 3440 (3463-23=3440) | | |

2 Kings 23:33–34: *"And Pharaoh-nechoh put him in bands at Riblah in the land of Hamath, that he might not reign in Jerusalem; And Pharaoh-nechoh made Eliakim the son of Josiah king in the room of Josiah his father, and turned his name to Jehoiakim, and took Jehoahaz away: and he came to Egypt, and died there."*

| 235. | Jehoahaz taken by Pharaoh Nechoh; died in Egypt | 3463 | 537 |

Pharaoh Nechoh came into dominion over the Jews decidedly but briefly. Babylon was the ascending power in the region, and within the beginning year of Jehoiakim's reign, Nebuchadnezzar, king of Babylon, *"came up."*

2 Kings 23:36: *"Jehoiakim was twenty and five years old when he began to reign; and he reigned eleven years in Jerusalem."*

(3463+11=3474) That is; Jehoiakim (Eliakim) reigned from 3463 to 3474.

| 236. | Jehoiakim (Eliakim) @ 25 begins 11-year reign | 3463 | 537 |
| | Jehoiakim born in 3438 (3463-25=3438) | | |

2 Kings 24:1: *"In his days Nebuchadnezzar king of Babylon came up, and Jehoiakim became his servant three years: then he turned and rebelled against him."*

(3463+3=3466)

237. Nebuchadnezzar begins reign as King of Bab-   3466   534
ylon; Jehoiakim refuses to heed the prophet's
warnings; the king of Babylon supplants the
king of Judah as per the judgment of God;
God's glory upon the nation departs; ending
of the 390 years of Ezek. 4:5

Regarding this end point of the 390 years of Ezek. 4:5: At the time of Nebuchadnezzar's ini- tial sole reign of Babylon, Israel had been in defeat, scattered, and humiliated for 114 years (3352 to 3466=114). The considerable part of Israel who ended up within the southern kingdom were under the same auspices and reproach. Nebuchadnezzar's beginning dominion and the provocation by Jehoiakim marked the end of any glory, control, or continuity of people. However much they were integrated into Judah's failing dominion, it ceased at that point. Jeremiah made that fact clear. Pos- sibly, the overriding consideration is that Nebuchadnezzar at that time became God's servant.

238. Jeremiah reflects on his warning   3467–<u>3468</u>   532

Jer. 25:1, 3, 11:

The word that came to Jeremiah concerning all the people of Judah in the <u>fourth year</u> of Jehoia- kim the son of Josiah king of Judah, that was the <u>first year of Nebuchadnezzar king of Babylon</u>.... From the <u>thirteenth year of Josiah</u> the son of Amon king of Judah, even unto this day, that is the <u>three and twentieth year</u>, the word of the LORD hath come unto me, and I have spoken unto you (Jehoiakim/Judah), rising early and speaking; but ye have not hearkened.... And this whole land shall be a desolation, and an astonishment; and these nations shall serve the king of Babylon <u>seventy years</u>.

(3432+13=3445) (3445+23=3468) (3463+4=3467)
2 Kings 24:1: *"In his days Nebuchadnezzar king of Babylon came up, and Jehoiakim became his ser- vant three years: then he turned and rebelled against him."*
(3463+3=3466) (3466+8=3474) (3463+11=3474)

239. Jehoakim rebels last 8 years of 11-year reign   3466 to <u>3474</u>   526

2 Kings 24:6: *"So Jehoiakim slept with his fathers: and Jehoiachin his son reigned in his stead."*

240. Jehoiakim died   3474   526

2 Kings 24:8: *"Jehoiachin was eighteen years old when he began to reign, and he reigned in Jerusalem three months."*

(3474+3 months=3474) That is: Jehoachin reigned in the year 3474.

| 241. | Jehoiachin @ 18 begins 3-month reign | 3474 | 526 |
| | Jehoiachin born in 3456 (3474-18=3456) | | |

2 Kings 24:10–15:

At that time the servants of Nebuchadnezzar king of Babylon came up against Jerusalem, and the city was besieged. And Nebuchadnezzar king of Babylon came against the city, and his servants did besiege it. And Jehoiachin the king of Judah went out to the king of Babylon, he, and his mother, and his servants, and his princes, and his officers: and the king of Babylon took him in the eighth year of his reign. And he carried out thence all the treasures of the house of the LORD, and the treasures of the king's house, and cut in pieces all the vessels of gold which Solomon king of Israel had made in the temple of the LORD, as the LORD had said. And he carried away all Jerusalem, and all the princes, and all the mighty men of valor, even ten thousand captives, and all the craftsmen and smiths: none remained save the poorest sort of the people of the land. And he carried away Jehoiachin to Babylon, and the king's mother, and the king's wives, and his officers, and the mighty of the land, those carried he into captivity from Jerusalem to Babylon.

That would be the eighth year of Nebuchadnezzar's reign. From 2 Kings 24:1 above, the first three years of Jehoiakim's eleven-year reign, he submitted to Babylonian rule. For the next eight years, he rebelled. Second Kings 24:2–4 depict a troubled time for Judah. Scripture indicates that during those eight years, the king of Babylon was entertaining other battlefronts. No doubt the Israeli scenario was a vexation that played out when Nebuchadnezzar gave it his attention.

It is no coincidence that Jehoiakim's rebellion against the king of Babylon coincided with Nebuchadnezzar's first eight-year sole reign in Babylon from 3466 to 3474.

Accordingly, after eight years of rebellion, Jehoiakim's reign ended, and his son, Jehoiachin, experienced a brief reign of three months.

| 242. | Begin 70 years of Babylonian captivity | 3474 | 526 |

2 Kings 24:17–18: *"And the king of Babylon made Mattaniah his father's* (Jehoiakim's) *brother king in his stead, and changed his name to Zedekiah. Zedekiah was twenty and one years old when he began to reign, and he reigned eleven years in Jerusalem."*

(3474+11=3485) That is: Zedekiah reigned from 3474 to 3485.

243. Zedekiah (Mattaniah) @ 21 begins 11-year   3474   526
      reign

Zedekiah continues as king, appointed by Nebuchadnezzar, but at a time when the continuity of the nation was exhausted. Nebuchadnezzar's patience was exhausted. Zedekiah's end was horrific. Jehoiachin's end of life was more pleasant.

244. *Salathiel, born of Jeconiah in captivity @ 21   estimated   3477   523

Ezek. 1:1–2: *"Now it came to pass in the thirtieth year, in the fourth month, in the fifth day of the month, as I was among the captives by the river of Chebar, that the heavens were opened, and I saw visions of God. In the fifth day of the month, which was the fifth year of king Jehoiachin's captivity."*

The fifth year of Jehoiachin's captivity would be the thirteenth year of Nebuchadnezzar's reign (3479-3466=13). The *"thirtieth"* should read "thirteenth," and that date refers to the reign of Nebuchadnezzar. (3466+13=3479) (3474+5=3479)

Ezek. 4:1–2, 5–6:

Thou also, son of man, take thee a tile, and lay it before thee, and pourtray upon it the city, even Jerusalem: And lay siege against it, and build a fort against it, and cast a mount against it; set the camp also against it, and set battering rams against it round about.... For I have laid upon thee the years of their iniquity, according to the number of the days, three hundred and ninety days: so shalt thou bear the iniquity of the house of Israel. And when thou hast accomplished them, lie again on thy right side, and thou shalt bear the iniquity of the house of Judah forty days: I have appointed thee each day for a year.

245. The 5th year of Jehoiachin's captivity,   3479   521
      Ezekiel prophesies of 390 days/years, and
      40 days/years

This prophecy and performance by Ezekiel demonstrated the 390 years regarding Israel, and the forty years regarding Judah. The prophecy related to the pending siege, which predated the siege by four years (3479–3483=4). As such, it was a near-end statement.

The dates of Nebuchadnezzar's arrival and the siege are given in 2 Kings 25:1–4, 8. Expressly: 10/10/9 to 4/9/11, and on to the occupation, 5/7/11. The setup and siege was eighteen months minus one day. (18 months x 30 days/month=540 days - 1 day=539 days) The occupation of Jerusalem concluded thirty-one days later. The total duration of the destruction operation was 570 days.

Additional to the application of Ezek. 4:5–6 to the siege, he is reflecting on the iniquity of Israel and Judah, totaling 430 years. That is: 390 years relating to Israel and forty years relating to Judah, "each day for a year." As it relates to the chronology and this prophecy, the time span of the forty years of iniquities was determined earlier in the chronology. That is 3445 to 3485. The 390-year time span was from 3076 to 3466.

2 Kings 25:1–4, 8:

And it came to pass in the <u>ninth year</u> of his (Zedekiah) reign, in the <u>tenth month</u>, in the <u>tenth day of the month</u>, that Nebuchadnezzar king of Babylon came, he, and all his host against Jerusalem, and pitched against it; and they built forts against it round about. And the city was besieged unto the eleventh year of King Zedekiah. And on the <u>ninth day of the fourth month</u> the famine prevailed in the city, and there was no bread for the people of the land. And the city was broken up.... And in the <u>fifth month, on the seventh day of the month</u>, which is the <u>nineteenth year</u> of king Nebuchadnezzar king of Babylon, came Nebuzaradan, captain of the guard, a servant of the king of Babylon, unto Jerusalem.

(3474+9=3483) (3474+11=3485) (3466+19=3485) (3466+19=3485)

246.   Jerusalem was besieged by Nebuchadnezzar; Jerusalem was besieged for about 1½ years and destroyed the 11th year of Zedekiah   3483   517

247.   Jerusalem was broken up and burned, taken and occupied; the men of war fled, and the walls and Temple torn down; this marked the end of the nation of Judah, including the remnant of Israel; end of 40 years of Ezek. 4:6   3485   515

The estimated year of birth of Salathiel and Pedaiah was determined by dividing the sixty-three-year difference between the estimated birth years of Jehoiachin and Zorobabel. (3456 to 3519=63) (63/3=21) (3456+21=3477 for Salathiel) (3477+21=3498 for Pedaiah)

248.   *Pedaiah, son born of Salathiel @ 21   estimated   3498   502

2 Kings 25:27–28: *"And it came to pass in the <u>seven and thirtieth year</u> of the captivity of Jehoiachin king of Judah, in the <u>twelfth month, on the seven and twentieth day</u> of the month, that Evil-merodach king of*

Babylon in the year that he began to reign did lift up the head of Jehoiachin king of Judah out of prison; And he spake kindly to him, and set his throne above the throne of the kings that were with him in Babylon."

3474+37=3511

249.	Evil-merodach, king of Babylon, began to reign Jehoiachin released from prison and exalted in Babylon 12/27		3511	489
250.	*Zorobabel born of Pedaiah @ 21	estimated	3519	481

"Zerubbabel the son of Shealtiel," Ezra 5:2, is the same Zorobabel, son (grandson) of Salathiel. He was instrumental early in the return to rebuild in Jerusalem, as per the decree of Cyrus in 3544. There is no given date of birth or death. He was of responsible age and likely a younger man. Only by conjecture and estimation can he be assigned the age of twenty-five at the time of the decree. His birth is thus given as the estimated year 3519 (3544-25=3519).

2 Chron. 36:18–21:

And all the vessels of the house of God, great and small, and the treasures of the house of the LORD, and the treasures of the king, and of his princes; all these he brought to Babylon. And they burnt the house of God, and brake down the wall of Jerusalem, and burnt all the palaces thereof with fire, and destroyed all the goodly vessels thereof. And them that had escaped from the sword carried he away to Babylon; where they were servants to him and his sons until the reign of the kingdom of Persia: To fulfil the word of the LORD by the mouth of Jeremiah, until the land had enjoyed her sabbaths: for as long as she lay desolate she kept sabbath, to fulfill threescore and ten years.

Jer. 25:11: *"And this whole land shall be a desolation, and an astonishment; and these nations shall serve the king of Babylon seventy years."*

Jer. 29:10: *"For thus saith the LORD, That after seventy years be accomplished at Babylon I will visit you, and perform my good word toward you, in causing you to return to this place."*

2 Kings 36:22–23:

Now in the first year of Cyrus king of Persia, that the word of the LORD spoken by the mouth of Jeremiah might be accomplished, the LORD stirred up the spirit of Cyrus king of Persia, that he made a proclamation throughout all his kingdom, and put it also in writing, saying, Thus saith Cyrus king of Persia, All the kingdoms of the earth hath the LORD God of heaven given me; and *he hath charged me to <u>build him an house in Jerusalem</u>, which is in Judah. Who is there among you of all his people? The LORD his God be with him, and let him go up.*

These scriptures give the seventy years' time accomplished in captivity, the ending of those seventy years' captivity as prophesied by Jeremiah, and the decree by Cyrus to rebuild in the city of Jerusalem, primarily the Temple. Restated: This ends the seventy years of Babylonian captivity and marks the year of Cyrus's decree: 3544 (3474+70=3544).

251.	Babylon falls to Darius of Media prophesied by Jeremiah Cyrus decrees a return to Jerusalem and to *"build him an house in Jerusalem,"* which begins the seventy weeks of years, equaling 490 years (Daniel 9:24–27); end of 70 years' Babylonian captivity; begin 490 years as prophesied	3544	456

Dan. 9:24–27:

<u>*Seventy weeks*</u> *are determined upon thy people and upon thy holy city, to finish the transgression, and to make an end of sins, and to make reconciliation for iniquity, and to bring in everlasting righteousness, and to seal up the vision and prophecy, and to anoint the most Holy. Know therefore and understand, that <u>from the going forth of the commandment to restore and to build Jerusalem unto the Messiah the Prince shall be seven weeks, and threescore and two weeks</u>: the street shall be built again, and the wall, even in troublous times. And <u>after threescore and two weeks shall Messiah be cut off</u>, but not for himself: and the people of the prince that shall come shall destroy the city and the sanctuary; and the end thereof shall be with a flood, and unto the end of the war desolations are determined. And <u>he shall confirm the covenant with many for one week; and in the midst of the week he shall cause the sacrifice and the oblation to cease,</u> and for the overspreading of abominations he shall make it desolate, even until the consummation, and that determined shall be poured upon the desolate.*

252.	That time span of 490 years is 3544 to 4034	3544	456

Beyond the birth date of either Jehoiachin or Jeconiah, taken to be 3456, no further dates are given to determine the years of birth for the lineage of Christ. As demonstrated, there is basis for the estimated year of birth Zorobabel, 3519. The count of years going forward from Zerubbabel's birth to the birth of Christ is 477 years. (3519 to 3996=477)

The text in Dan. 9:24–27 includes the prophesied 483 years from the decree of Cyrus, 3544, to the beginning of Christ's ministry with Jesus being *"about thirty years of age"* (Luke 3:23). Subtracting the "about thirty years" from 483 gives a time of 453 years (483-30=453) from Cyrus's decree to Christ's birth. That would be 3544+453=3997; call it 3996. The year of Zorobabel's birth is estimated to be 3519. That birth was estimated to be twenty-five years prior to the captivity (3544 to 3519=25). Therefore, the time span from Zorobabel's birth to Jesus' birth would be the 453-year figure plus twenty-five years, or 478 years (453+25=478).

To get estimated, averaged dates for the births of Christ's lineage, going forward, including Zorobabel, we need the number of individuals involved so that we can divide 568 years by that number minus one. Matt. 1:17 states fourteen generations: *"From the carrying away into Babylon unto Christ are fourteen generations."* Fourteen individuals from Jeconiah to Christ. Our calculation starts less Salathiel and Pedaiah; so that the number is twelve. Dividing 478 by twelve minus one or eleven, we calculate about 43½ years per generation (478/11=43½). To avoid the use of fractions of years, we alternate with the years forty-three and forty-four years per generation to get the estimated birth dates. This determination is given and listed as such in the table. However, it is understood that the forty-three to forty-four years between generations is tacit. The chart Christ's Lineage; Old Testament Record, Matt. 1 and Luke 3 is given for the very reason of demonstrating that Matt. 1:1–17 leaves out six, then about nine persons, in this case, whose addition would render the generations separated by a more reasonable approximation of twenty-five years; not forty-three to forty-four years.

253.	*Abiud born 3519+43=3562	estimate +43	3562	438
254.	*Eliakim born 3562+43=3605	estimate +43	3605	395
255.	*Azor born 3605+44=3649	estimate +44	3649	351
256.	*Sadoc born 3649+43=3692	estimate +43	3692	308
257.	*Achim born 3692+44=3736	estimate +44	3736	264
258.	*Eliud born 3736+43=3779	estimate +43	3779	221

259.	*Eleazar born 3779+44=3823	estimate +44	3823	177
260.	*Matthan born 3823+43=3866	estimate +43	3866	134
261.	*Jacob born 3866+44=3910	estimate +44	3910	90
262.	*Joseph born 3910+43=3953	estimate +43	3953	47
263.	*Jesus born 3953+43=3996	estimate +43	3996	4

SEVENTH ERA	4000	4000	0

Dan. 9:25 gives the time intervals, *"Seven weeks, and threescore and two weeks."* Sixty-nine weeks of years totals 483 years. Beginning with Cyrus's decree in 3544, the 483 years takes us to 4027 (3544+483=4027)

264.	Jesus baptized in Jordan	4027	27 AD

Beginning the last week of the seventy weeks and going forward: *"And he shall confirm the covenant with many for one week: and in the midst of the week he shall cause the sacrifice and the oblation to cease"* (Dan. 9:27). Jesus ministered for 3½ years.

After ministering 3½ years, until the middle of the 70th week, he is crucified, fulfilling the Pascal sacrifice and oblation so that animal-sacrifice loses its efficacy. It ceases.

Regarding the 70th week to commensurate with Dan. 9:27 is Dan. 12:6–7: *"And one said to the man clothed in linen, which was upon the waters of the river, How long shall it be to the end of these wonders? And I heard the man clothed in linen, which was upon the waters of the river, when he held up his right hand and his left hand unto heaven, and sware by him that liveth for ever that it shall be for a time, times, and an half; and when he shall have accomplished to scatter the power of the holy people, all these things shall be finished."*

"Time" is one year. "Times" is two years, and "an half" is one-half year. The total is 3½ years. That would be the first half of Daniel's 70th week.

265.	Jesus crucified, great earthquake, resurrection	4030	30 AD

266.   *Generation of Christ born at Pentecost;   4030   30 AD
        the Church comes into existence

This is Christ's generation. The Church and Apostles of the Church began ministering the last message of truth to the Jews for 3½ years, thus concluding the 70th week of Daniel's seventy weeks. The last 3½ ends, *"When he shall have accomplished to <u>scatter</u> the <u>power</u> of the holy people"* (Dan. 12:7). That "scatter" corresponds to the time of the stoning of Stephen. *"And Saul was consenting unto his (Stephen's) death. And at that time there was a great persecution against the church which was at Jerusalem; and they were <u>scattered</u> abroad throughout the regions of Judaea and Samaria, except the apostles"* (Acts 8:1). Also, Acts 11:19: *"Now they which were <u>scattered</u> abroad upon the persecution that arose about Stephen travelled as far as Phenice, and Cyprus, and Antioch, <u>preaching the word</u> to none but unto the Jews only."*

The expression "scatter the power" would necessarily refer to the mentioned preaching of God's word. The apostle Paul states in Rom. 1:16: *"For I am not ashamed of the gospel of Christ: for it is the <u>power</u> of God unto salvation."*

That last half of the week of the 3½ years saw the "second witness" ministry of the early Church. Heb. 2:3 says, *"How shall we escape, if we neglect so great salvation; which at the <u>first</u> began to be spoken by the LORD, and was <u>confirmed</u> unto us by them that heard him;"* That ends with the stoning of Stephen. The last week is thus fulfilled and the seventy weeks is completed in the year 4034 (4027+7=4034).

267.   Stephen was stoned and the people scattered;   4034   34 AD
        Dan. 12:7; Acts 8:1,4; 11:19;
        End of 490 years of Dan. 9:24–27

Postscript

PROPHETIC STATEMENTS OF SCRIPTURE have a duality of purpose and fulfillment. Beyond the "literal" fulfillment of the 70th week, there may be "spiritual" fulfillment. The point in question: We are led to the understanding of a "gap," with a near-future fulfillment of the last 3½ years; Some say seven years. As perceived, the gap would be the same "great gulf" of Luke 16:26; the "until" of Rom. 11:25, and the time of "the veil" (2 Cor. 3:16). If there is an "overlay" and it registers, and if that is a reality, then there is yet to transpire an end-time latter rain ministry of 3½ years: As pertaining to the Jews' past; so pertaining more currently to the Gentiles. The relating prophecy often brought to bear is Hosea 6:2, *"After two days will he revive us: in the third day he will raise us up, and we shall live in his sight."*

Concerning the above prophecy and the matter of Christ's return and associated phenomena: Two thousand years added to the year 34 AD gives a date of 2034 AD. There is great danger in managing numbers, even worse, manipulating numbers. That landscape is fraught with pitfalls. This chronology does not deny, nor does it lend itself to such prognosticating. TFI.